DYSLEXIA

A Universe of Possibilities

Elizabeth Cottone, PhD

DYSLEXIA

A UNIVERSE OF POSSIBILITIES

ELIZABETH COTTONE PHD

4 PEAS PRESS

ISBN 978-1-0879-8624-1

Library of Congress Control Number 2021918423

4 Peas Press, Charlottesville, Virginia

Cover drawing by Dahlia Becker

Umbrella drawing, sandpaper letters, and Touch Math numerals by Cecilia Becker

Author photos by Mary Catherine Cottone (with donkey), Cecilia Becker (portrait), and Gail Todter (horseback)

Visit the author's website at elizabethcottone.com

CONTENTS

This book is for all those individuals, old and young,
who are brilliant and yet cannot tie their shoes.

ACKNOWLEDGMENTS

I am indebted to the young student I call "Mike," and his whole family. Without knowing Mike or working with him on his reading, writing, and study skills as well as his emotional development, I never would have written this book. I am also indebted to the older student I call "Steve," for sharing his experiences with ADHD (differences that mostly present as high intelligence alongside severe disorganization and inattention) in high school and college. He was open about his ADHD, and supportive of me during my stroke recovery. I feel honored to have met him.

I thank Dr. Sally Shaywitz for her work at the Yale Center for Creativity and Dyslexia, and especially for her insightful book called *Overcoming Dyslexia*.[1] Both a great read and reference on dyslexia, it inspired me to write this book. I also thank Robin Hegner for her great work unraveling the meaning and definition of ADHD as well as its warning signs, and Tom West for his wonderful book about the strengths of dyslexia, entitled *In the Mind's Eye*.[2]

I would also like to acknowledge Mike's parents "Emily" and "Keith" for all the hard work they have put in to helping Mike, as well as the time they have put into helping me with this book. As the parents, they must have had a hard time raising Mike—I can only imagine—even though he's a great child. But the rewards will be huge, no doubt.

Finally, I would like to thank Dr. Julie Blodgett, who as a friend, colleague, and support system for many years, has helped me so much, not only with this book, but with many other personal and professional obstacles.

FOREWORD

I have known and admired Beth Cottone since she was a PhD student in our program at the University of Virginia. I admired not only her many other fine personal qualities but the fact that she is "the real deal." She is a scholar, but not the "ivory tower" type. She knows kids. She knows how to teach kids.

Beth draws on her many years of teaching and administering programs for students with a variety of disabilities as well as her "hands-on" experience in research. Unlike many people with advanced degrees, she knows whereof she speaks, whether she is speaking or writing about children and education. She can say about more things than most of her colleagues, "been there, done that."

With her stroke, Beth has found a silver lining, in that it has given her a first-hand perspective on the struggles that many children and youths face in learning. She now sees disabilities more clearly and personally than before. However, Beth was a brilliant scholar-teacher before her stroke, and it did not take a cerebrovascular accident (CVA, as strokes are sometimes called) to make her understand or be sensitive to children's learning problems. Furthermore, she is not among the lunatic fringe who think disabilities are good things to have, should be cele-brated, or—in the other extreme—don't really matter.

This book is something to be celebrated. It is full of wisdom about how to help kids with disabilities, especially the reading difficulty called dyslexia. If I had a child with dyslexia, I would want Beth to teach him or her. And, if I couldn't have Beth be the teacher, I would want the teacher to read this book and learn from Beth's wisdom.

James M. Kauffman
Professor Emeritus of Education
University of Virginia
June, 2021

PREFACE

Dyslexia is considered to be a significant impediment to academic achievement in school, and is accompanied by negative emotional consequences as well. But it is important to remember and highlight the many nonlinear strengths that people with dyslexia possess, including high levels of cognition, logic, creativity, and skill at drawing conclusions. Unfortunately, these individuals are heavily penalized by their main weakness: phonological awareness (PA), a person's understanding of the sound structures of words within language, regardless of the words' meaning. People with dyslexia are often brilliant in other areas—such as making comparisons and thinking outside the box—but these strengths are often overlooked due to our educational system's overreliance on the gateway skill of PA.

PA has become so essential to success in elementary school in the United States that even very bright and talented children with dyslexia can find themselves failing. In fact, that one skill is necessary but not sufficient for a student to be successful in school. The student must be able to read, and then think critically and creatively, not just read by word-calling or decoding (breaking apart a word, then saying it correctly, with no understanding of its meaning). If a student has the ability to build a persuasive argument, then that student has shown an ability to think deeply about a topic, which is surely more valuable than just reading the words.

Hecht and colleagues investigated verbal number codes in their study examining whether children's phonological processes (phonological memory, rate of access, and PA) in second grade were associated with mathematical computation skills through fifth grade.[1] They found that second grade PA accounted for 10% of the variance in fifth grade math computation skills, thus supporting the potential for a common cognitive pathway between reading and math computation. They claimed that since children routinely convert the terms of the mathematical problems into speech sounds before solving it, phonological processes can serve to moderate this process, thus aiding or inhibiting the success of the solution.[2]

Dyslexia has been known as the invisible disability and, though a bit cliché, the name is appropriate. The disorder is as painful as it is, particularly in the United States, partly because people with dyslexia look exactly the same as those without it.

The pain of having dyslexia also results partly from the overemphasis on PA. It is a precursor to reading, and is thus important, but when PA is the only significant area of weakness, all of the other areas of cognition are intact—and are usually advanced—in people with dyslexia. These other areas include high levels of cognitive leaping, reasoning, and arguing constructively.

So, for the person with dyslexia, school can be difficult because it often overemphasizes PA as well as the organizational skills that elude students with dyslexia and attention-deficit hyperactivity disorder (ADHD). ADHD occurs when an individual has great difficulty staying organized, paying attention to the expected focus, is more impulsive than most, and is hyperactive. It is neurodevelopmental in nature and often, but not always, comes along with dyslexia. If they are able to successfully complete school, these students can thrive, because their strengths in advanced reasoning and critical thinking are more likely to be tapped in adult life—which is when the silver lining is easier to perceive.

Dyslexia can be painful and embarrassing. Like stroke survivors, individuals with dyslexia are often misunderstood. People who work with them and/or are close to them must "get" them, recognize their brilliant mind, and understand how their brain works...which is not easy and is often uncomfortable. But they must appreciate that these people with dyslexia are often very smart. We must turn to them and celebrate their out-of-the-box thinking instead of punishing them for failing or acting impulsively or not getting into the college we may want them to. These are truly amazing individuals with exceptional strengths to offer.

I have a strong background, both practical and academic, in dyslexia. Both my master's and PhD are in Learning Disabilities, and I have trained three times in the Orton-Gillingham philosophy, taught by three different experts. (I wanted to be thoroughly prepared to teach different students, and I was interested to see how the three trainings compared.) From this background, I created my own reading and study skills curricula and have had great success with them, with all of my students with dyslexia.

The relationship between the student and teacher is an important part of the student's development. I am committed to each student's unique path toward learning, and I have applied and adapted specific approaches to meet each student's needs. Throughout my master's and PhD programs—and my entire working life—I tutored children with dyslexia, even while being employed full time. I learned so much and continue to learn so much from my students.

An unexpected development in my own life also informs this book. In 2017, I had a massive cerebellar, hemorrhagic stroke. It almost killed me. I lost a lot, including my work as an educational researcher and tutor, my running career, my tennis playing, and most importantly, my ability to take care of my three daughters and my animals. I knew I needed to be grateful to be alive, but I often felt sad and frustrated. It was hard to have a stroke, but I have certainly learned a lot and it has changed me for the better.

ADHD comes into play in the later chapters of this book. As with dyslexia, ADHD tends to present in bright, curious students, and can exist with or without hyperactivity. I have come to see that dyslexia, ADHD, and certain types of stroke share many similarities as well as some differences.

I learned true empathy as a result of my stroke and rehabilitation. It is so painful to make a switch from teacher to student, but it's also full of silver linings. One is that very few people can truly understand both perspectives. This is very advantageous for the student with dyslexia because there is a lot to understand, including the emotional fallout that inevitably happens. Another is the feeling of real empathy that is irreplaceable once one has walked some miles in another's shoes. It's important to have empathy for everyone, but especially so for the individual with dyslexia because, unlike many others around them, these individuals have often had years of failure and degradation. As a result, they are very sensitive and angry, rightly so. During the years of my recovery, I can appreciate even more the struggles as well as the stepwise solutions that are now available to people with different brains.

Elizabeth Cottone PhD
Charlottesville, Virginia
August, 2021

INTRODUCTION

I am not fully healed, I
am not fully wise,
I am still on my way.
What matters is that
I am moving forward
—Yung Pueblo, *Inward*

This book is for anyone who cares about struggling and slow readers; in other words, readers with dyslexia. It is important to note that dyslexia is a neurological difference, not a manmade construct. This means that individuals with dyslexia have a neurological difference that causes the overt symptoms we see, as opposed to the manner in which we measure it. I have had many direct experiences with bright children who struggle with reading, avoid print, and read slowly, if at all. Some of them become very accomplished adults and some end up in jail. Through science and a strengths-based approach, we have great hope that we can solve this problem and remediate the difficulties that haunt those with dyslexia. Having been in the field of dyslexia for almost thirty years, and having taught many students with dyslexia successfully, I care deeply about people with this condition. I am convinced that, given the appropriate education, they can overcome their brain-based difficulties and mature into creative adult lives, excelling in unique ways.

My educational philosophy and practice stem from my vision for re-educating all aspects of the individual with dyslexia. I maintain a deep optimism about the uniquely creative contributions these students make to society, and the capacity they possess not only for academic success, but also for lifelong fulfillment. My philosophy centers on the notion that a well-trained team of educators can work together to produce monumental change across multiple dimensions of each child. Below I describe what I feel are the components necessary for this change to occur.

Create the Right Context for Learning

The thread that weaves through all of my professional experiences, from teacher to administrator to researcher, is my commitment to attaining success with students who fall outside the bell curve. The seeds of my approach were planted more than twenty years ago at a small private school in the Northeast for children with dyslexia. As an assistant teacher, I observed the founder and director, who had dyslexia, tirelessly guide staff through long training sessions, passionately but precisely conveying exactly what the child with dyslexia was feeling, how they saw the world, and how they should be educated.

From that moment forward, I recognized the importance of managing the instructional context of the learner with dyslexia so as to create the right environment for high-quality teaching and learning to occur. I came to recognize that small contexts with highly trained educators unencumbered by bureaucratic rules and structure provide the ideal setting to educate the child with dyslexia.

Empower with Foundational and Qualitatively Different
Instruction

Today, I embrace a strengths-based approach with a whole-child focus, grounded in the belief that teaching children with dyslexia begins with a strong foundation in basic academic skills. New-found successes in the areas of reading, writing, and math may then have a bootstrapping effect on emotional and interpersonal growth.

My theoretical training and direct experience with children with dyslexia have consistently shown me that the Orton-Gillingham (OG) approach to language instruction (or similar programs that are direct, structured, multisensory, and phonologically based) is essential for remediating and solidifying basic reading and writing skills. This instruction enables students to rebuild the foundation of reading and writing, thereby creating new circuitry in the brain that results in lasting change. The teaching and modeling of crucial organizational and study skills can become natural next steps in a complete approach to working with the population with dyslexia.

My 20 years with the OG method have led me to recognize that while this approach is critical, it is only part of the instructional story for children with dyslexia, who negotiate all aspects of the world from a different perspective. Self- awareness, self- reflection, and ultimately self-acceptance are important components that can be modeled and taught directly. As with all students who span a range of learning profiles, an honest acceptance of strengths and limitations only increases the ability of each child to become their own advocate. This holistic approach, in combination with a solid academic base, engenders feelings of emotional and interpersonal competence, thus increasing overall self-confidence and a feeling of empowerment to move through the world.

Cultivate the Unique Strengths of an Exceptional Population

Students with dyslexia are undoubtedly unique with a great deal to offer the world. I have found nothing to compare to the spirit and personality, as well as the exceptional perspectives and thought processes that characterize this population. The "splinter skills" (those areas of extreme talent or giftedness) that characterize many children with dyslexia draw me to them the most. I am humbled and amazed by the areas—most often spatial and artistic—in which these children excel, but I'm also dismayed that these are not the areas that traditional schooling celebrates.

Conventional education is linear and linguistic in its focus, and it is troubling to think that a child with language-based deficits may feel that their weaknesses are constantly highlighted, so that they become convinced that these qualities are the only ones of value in our society. These children need to be fully recognized for their spatial and creative strengths, and their education must tap all parts of the brain, thus uncovering the exceptional skills they possess.

Build a Bridge to Continued Success

As an educator of children with dyslexia, I often think of a bridge-building metaphor. A well- built bridge closes gaps and expands into new territories. The bridge we build creates a different pathway, ending in a new and better place, unlike the previously travelled terrain that was often filled with failure, ridicule, and misunder-standing.

As a bridge builder, an educator's perspective must acknowledge where each student has come from, where they are at the present moment, and where they are going. A constant telescoping of view, in and out, is the only way for the educator to ensure that the bridge leads down the right path for each student.

The bridge has multiple levels: it leads to academic success, emotional and interpersonal fulfillment, and self-acceptance. It enables students to recognize where and how they fit best within the world, and how much they have to offer.

The bridge is always under close maintenance and at times, under construction. As its builders, we benefit greatly from our own experience as well as from the ongoing learning, research, and professional development that uncover knowledge about the richness and complexity of the structure and processing of the mind with dyslexia.

The bridge takes students to a place of self-knowledge of their gifts and strengths, and an empowered recognition that their weaknesses, once incapacitating and overwhelming, can be conquered with the right instruction, guidance, and perspective. The bridge leads students back into a part of the mainstream for which they are now fully equipped, confident about rejoining, and excited about discovering its adventures and challenges.

HOW TO USE THIS BOOK

Every other chapter in DYSLEXIA: A UNIVERSE OF POSSIBILITIES follows two students from pre-birth through college, with details of their strengths and struggles. The alternating chapters are more theoretical and technical, concerning the history, definition, warning signs of, assessment of, and the long-term outcomes for dyslexia and, in later chapters, attention-deficit hyperactivity disorder (ADHD).

Part One focuses on dyslexia and follows Emily and her son, Mike.[1] Both have dyslexia, and the majority of the book concerns Mike, dyslexia, and the struggles he encounters as a result of his dyslexia. I hope that everyone reads about Mike. Those students with dyslexia may relate to him, feel less alone, and empathize with his struggles. For others, it is important to read these chapters because they will provide a thorough description of exactly what it feels like to grow up with dyslexia. The other chapters are more theoretical and are for the person who may be interested in learning more about the definition of dyslexia as well as how it fits in with other learning disabilities, and how to teach the individual with dyslexia.

Part Two expands the discussion to include aspects of ADHD—following some of Steve's experiences—and of stroke, sharing some of my own story as a stroke survivor. We look at how dyslexia and ADHD may overlap. Most importantly, as with dyslexia, I explain the definition of ADHD, and provide an illustration of how it affected a real person.

The chapters and the entire book are purposely strengths-based, short, and relatively easy to read, in hopes that the readership will include students with dyslexia. The book contains good information for students, their families, and professionals and is intended to serve a wide audience. It will be both valuable and enjoyable to anyone who knows someone with dyslexia or ADHD, and wants to understand them better, or to the actual person with dyslexia or ADHD.

PART ONE • DYSLEXIA

(EMILY AND MIKE)

1 PARENTS AND HERITABILITY

The universe is full of magical things
patiently waiting for our wits to grow sharper.
—Eden Phillpotts, *A Shadow Passes*

Emily was born in 1967 and had dyslexia herself. She was diagnosed in third grade, by chance. The year was 1975, which just happened to be the year that an important federal law went into effect. "Until Congress passed the Education for All Handicapped Children act (Public Law 94-142) in 1975, kids with disabilities didn't even have a right to a free, appropriate public education."[1]

The new law supported more than 1 million children with disabilities who had been excluded entirely from the education system. The law had an ongoing ripple effect as well. When I was the director of a tutoring center for children with learning challenges, I can't tell you how many times I talked to parents who diagnosed their own learning disabilities through their children. These parents had also struggled to read, and discovered late in life that they themselves had dyslexia. Emily found out about dyslexia in her son "Mike" by comparing him to herself. (I tutored Mike for seven years, and, with his family's permission, will discuss his progress herein.) In Emily's own words, speaking about her diagnosis:

It just so happened that the lady next door, who was a good friend of my parents, was going to school to get a degree in special education. For this she needed to find kids and test them for learning disabilities. She conscripted most [of] the kids in the neighborhood. I was the one who stuck out. My skill pattern was a lot like my son Mike's but much less extreme. His score range was from K to 9th grade.[2]

I'm the youngest of two kids. My brother is five years older than I am. He doesn't have learning disabilities. Before the diagnosis, my parents were concerned and confused. I was a very bright, observant kid. I seem[ed] to know everything that was taught at school and I contributed a lot in class, but I did terribly on the tests. Spelling and writing were the worst.

Dyslexia is hereditary and is passed down from one generation to another at a rate of 80%. Emily's mom also had dyslexia. She passed dyslexia down to Emily who passed it on to Mike. This is very common. Emily's public school was not very understanding about her dyslexia. In fact, it often made her feel stupid or as if there was some-thing wrong with her. I can completely understand this, having gone to an all-girls Catholic school for 13 years! Though different from the public system, my school was equally rigid and harsh about reading. We used phonics workbooks that were hard and boring at the same time. I remember the lines in those workbooks didn't give us enough space to write out our answers. And anytime I erased, I would rip the paper. Somehow, we learned to read and write.

Looking back on that now, I can see how hard and grueling it would have been if I had had dyslexia. As a thrice-trained reading tutor, with a strong background in the Orton-Gillingham (OG) philosophy, a master's and PhD in special education, and a desire to improve on the OG method by developing my own curriculum for reteaching the foundation of reading, I fully understand how difficult these phonics books were. The child with dyslexia needed a qualitatively different approach to teaching reading, writing, and pretty much any content area.

Muscling through will only get you so far. It's about re-learning and re-building. This requires a slowness, which can be hard but necessary so you can really re-learn. When you go fast, you often skip steps, which undermines flexibility and creates holes in the foundation. The way I describe it to my students with dyslexia is that we are re-building a foundation and we want a firm and well-built foundation. If we don't have this, everything can crumble. Many are condemned to about a fourth-grade level, because that is as far as "muscling it" can take you.

Emily grew up during a time when women were not supposed to be smart anyway. Everything was very traditional back then, particularly male and female work and home roles, but Emily felt especially ill equipped for the small female workforce. Nonetheless, Emily pursued both her undergraduate degree and an MBA from a reputable institution. She landed a great job, and during her career, had three children. As with many people with dyslexia, including her son Mike, Emily excelled at conceptualizing numbers, science, and finance, but struggled with detailed problem solving in those realms. Again, in Emily's own words:

My mother was very engaged in finding out what was up, my father not so much. My mother struggled with some level of dyslexia herself, particularly in terms of spelling, so she was more "clued in" and empathetic before and after the diagnosis.

After the diagnosis, she went into action. I had lots of tutors and more than my fair share of summer school. I also changed schools, leaving the "open classroom" and my public school for the eagle eye supervision of the local Catholic school. It was a jolt. I was really far behind the other kids. I don't remember any accommodations. Rather, my mother's rule was: people judge your work on the end product. If it takes you twice as long to get to an appropriate outcome, (an A or B+) then that's what you do. My mother never earned lower than an A- in her entire academic career: college, then a master's program (a school in Chicago), a fellowship (a London school focusing on Economics) so the B+ was a big concession on her part. So, that was the set expectation: I was to get good grades, and if that meant I had to work twice as hard, well, so be it.

My parents did, however, do everything in their power to make it easier for me. They spent lots of time on teaching me how to structure an essay, editing papers, finding tutors, and generally keeping up my morale. In 1985, when I entered college, they bought me, at great expense, ($3,000) one of the first 'portable' (40 lbs) computers on the market. It was my lifesaver!

Also, Emily's mother was very clear that school was a phase, a bump in the road, and that once she had finished it, dyslexia would become a great strength, that she would be fine thereafter. Emily was a "people person," which was a great strength that other kids didn't have and that couldn't be learned. Emily said,

---

All I had to do is educate myself out of having to do administrative tasks… I needed to do well enough that I could get a job with a secretary!

It was that goal that motivated me during most of my high school, college and master's degree. (Of course, the early parts of this timeframe were before accommodations like computing and spellcheck - so the goal was more compelling.)

Away from home, support for her dyslexia was generally lacking.

The rest of the world was ignorant about my dyslexia and turned school into a pretty demoralizing experience. I think that many people with dyslexia encounter this choppy level of support: unconditional support from some people, a skeptical reception from others, and straight-out denial from the largest cohort.

At home, her two parents approached Emily's dyslexia differently.

My mother took the challenge head on; my father didn't engage (although he helped me a great deal in other parts of my education).

It wasn't until the summer after my graduation from college that my father engaged on the subject. We had a lock down drag out fight over my inability to memorize a set of directions to a place in Boston. I kept asking him if he'd slow down so I could write it down and he kept telling me I should be able to remember them. It got really nasty.

When we cooled down and did a 'post mortem,' he finally admitted that he'd never engaged on the subject because it upset him so much. How could his genetic offspring be so impaired? He took it as a personal affront that he had 'a kid like that.' He felt if he could instill intellectual discipline in me the dyslexia would go away. (I should mention that he's a political theory professor with a bent toward ancient Greek philosophy.

Much of my upbringing was based on Aristotle's views on child rearing.)
That evening he felt my inability to remember the directions was due to a
lack of intellectual discipline—if I would just try harder or focus more I
could do it. I responded that I had discipline. Indeed, I had just graduated
from one of the top 10 liberal arts colleges in the country 'with
distinction,' and I was in no humor to hear that I had a flabby mind. Also,
I said that I didn't hold him responsible for my dyslexia—it was not his
fault. Somehow that stopped him in his tracks. He apologized and since
then he's been really supportive of me; and Mike.

For a young person, a parent's approval is extremely important. It must have been very difficult for Emily to live with her father's distaste for dyslexia. This must have been similar for Mike, who clearly had trouble measuring up as compared to his siblings.

Keith, Mike's father, was born in 1967, and was the eldest of four children. He did not have dyslexia and had a very different experience growing up as compared to Emily. Nonetheless he was very involved in Mike's life—his tutoring, testing, schooling, and hobbies.

> *There is a crack ... in everything.*
> *That's how the light gets in.*
> —Leonard Cohen, "Anthem"

Mike is sandwiched between two very high-achieving siblings. His older brother used to go to the same private school as Mike before he transferred to a prestigious boarding school in New England. Mike's younger sister comprehended high and early, and has received good grades her whole life in the same private school that Mike attends. I can only imagine how hard all of that was for Mike, and his mother probably went through it too with her brother. I was also sandwiched between two very high-achieving siblings who went to the same school as me, so I felt stupid and was demoralized. I always thought my teachers, and sometimes even my friends, compared me negatively to my sisters. So I acted differently. I excelled in sports and drank too much. But I was lucky because my sports got me far, attracting lots of positive recognition. In Mike's case—and probably Emily's too—he was very, very smart! Maybe the smartest of all the children, but grades did not show this!

My husband Larry and I first met Emily and Keith before we had any children. Each couple had a dog. We met at an outdoor coffee cart and immediately became friends. Later, Emily and Larry would work together at a prestigious business school. There was nothing about Emily that suggested she had anything like dyslexia. She was poised and articulate—I did not sense any word-finding problems. At the time I don't think they knew I was studying dyslexia or anything having to do with education.

So we left our first encounter with Emily and Keith feeling quite good! We enjoyed them immensely and though we were just about to leave for our honeymoon in New Orleans, we knew we'd stay in touch. And we sure did, for many years and in contexts no one could have predicted. Later we would each have our oldest child at about the same time and though they were different genders—Emily and Keith had a boy and we had a girl—they became friends and went to the same day care center.

We proceeded to follow closely Emily and Keith with our second and third child. Larry and I have three girls and Emily and Keith have two boys and one girl. In both of our families, our middle child was and continues to be the one with the most issues that don't match well with the world. It was when my middle child was in second grade that I began my tutoring with Mike and shortly thereafter I learned about Emily's dyslexia.

———————

Dyslexia is a spectrum—a continuum. It is not black and white nor is it a categorical concept. Mike was definitely at the far end of the spectrum. In other words, he had severe dyslexia, and Emily probably did too. After working with Mike for about seven-and-a-half years, and being there for him during some difficult times, I felt that I really understood him and the dyslexia.

I have worked with many students who fall at various points on the continuum. I know the many different kinds of dyslexia that can exist. Each person is different and though, as this book suggests, there are commonalities that are important to thoroughly understand—like the OG philosophy that helps most individuals with dyslexia learn to read —it is necessary for every teacher and tutor to know their students really well, and to fully comprehend that every student is unique. I learned this from Mike and my other students, whom I admire. I think and hope that one day their amazing strengths will be recognized and celebrated.

I've also worked with and known students who are less severely affected. They are easier to work with cognitively, but can be equally as challenging as their peers who have more severe dyslexia, and can be more difficult emotionally than their peers, depending on IQ. I have found that the most difficult student to teach is the one we call "twice exceptional"—the student with an IQ in the gifted range who also has dyslexia. These students, like Mike, get very frustrated and have low self-esteem because they are smart enough to know what they don't know and are aware of their mistakes.

My children will often ask, "Mom, you love your students, don't you? Do you wish we had dyslexia?" I respond saying, "Yes, I do love my students and can recognize that they have great strengths. But no, I certainly don't wish my children had dyslexia because I know how hard and devastating it can be. And I wouldn't wish it on anyone."

I can imagine that as an intelligent girl with dyslexia, especially before 1975, Emily must have been very frustrated. Even after 1975, Emily must have been frustrated. And while times have definitely changed since 1975, they have not changed enough for the person with dyslexia.

Now, with dyslexia, still there is a great deal of misunderstanding. Similar to a person with a certain kind of stroke or with attention-deficit hyperactivity disorder (ADHD), the person with dyslexia may feel trapped and misunderstood. They may feel as though people are overgeneralizing and judging them as not very bright due to the struggle they have with reading. Sadly, they may be right. However, these students are often much brighter than those who judge them. Hopefully, this book will clarify to everyone how smart these individuals are and the misunderstanding and accompanying frustration will be alleviated.

2 WHAT IS DYSLEXIA? WHY SHOULD WE CARE?

Obstacles do not block the path;
they are the path.
—Zen proverb

What Is Dyslexia?

Unlike language or some aspects of math, reading is not naturally wired in the brain.

The idea that every child learns to read easily is simply not true. Dyslexia is when reading is hard, slow, laborious, and not fun. It has its roots in the linguistic system, is lifelong, and is complex. It disrupts the neural system that codes language. We have come to understand how this neural "glitch" reaches beyond reading and affects spelling, word retrieval, articulation, and memory. With the advances of technology, we can now "see" reading in the brain. According to Dr. Sally Shaywitz in *Overcoming Dyslexia*, "By identifying the primary or core cognitive weakness responsible for dyslexia, scientists now understand how children acquire the ability to read and why some do not. ... [A] person's ability to read is routed through the same pathway [as everyone else's] deep within the brain. This pathway has been identified."[1]

Dyslexia is a specific learning disability that is neurobiological in origin. It is characterized by difficulties with accurate and/or fluent word recognition and by poor spelling and decoding abilities. These difficulties typically result from a deficit in the phonological component of language that is often unexpected in relation to other cognitive abilities and the provision of effective classroom instruction. Secondary consequences may include problems in reading comprehension and reduced reading experience that can impede growth of vocabulary and background knowledge.[2]

Phonological awareness (PA) is an oral language precursor to reading that focuses on the ability to hear and manipulate the sounds within words irrespective of the meaning of the word.[3] Examples of PA skills include rhyming, alliteration, elision, blending, and segmenting words into individual speech sounds.[4] In normally developing children, mastering the rules and patterns of this segmentation happens at around age 6, though the range is wide, with successful PA skills identified in children as young as two years and as old as age 8.[5]

> *Real empathy is sometimes not insisting*
> *that it will be ok, but acknowledging that it is not.*
> —Sheryl Sandberg, Online Counseling College blog

Four decades of research have shown that the more sensitive children are to the segmented parts of words, the more success they will have as readers, regardless of intelligence, vocabulary, or socioeconomic status.[6]Successful matching of the segmented speech sounds to the printed word begins the process of "cracking the code" of reading. Since the nature of reading is based in the alphabetic principle (one or several letters represent a single speech sound), PA in tandem with letter name knowledge and letter sound knowledge has been shown by many to be highly predictive of later reading skill.[7] Unlike language, for many children, PA is not a naturally developing ability. It requires direct exposure and practice opportunity. This malleability and sensitivity to instruction is encouraging and suggests the importance of effective, research-based instruction in PA as early as preschool.[8] Professionals unanimously agree that preschool PA instruction helps to alleviate difficulties later and minimize the number of students with reading issues throughout the primary grades.[9]

While almost all children have the capacity to develop PA, certain groups vary in the skill level, age, and rate at which mastery occurs.[10] Extensive research over the past few decades has shown that students with reading difficulties have core deficits in the area of PA and similar language processing skills.[11] Children from households with lower income and education also reflect a persistent gap in PA skill level as compared to those with higher income and education. Henning and colleagues pose that this connection between low PA and low socioeconomic status is associated with lower oral language development as well as vocabulary usage.[12] Environments that are under-enriched for language have a deleterious effect on all aspects of literacy, but most critically on the code-related aspects, including PA.[13] While children who live in households that meet the federal criteria for poverty look very similar to children with language impairments,[14] having both of these risk factors exacerbates the effect on PA development. Therefore, children who fall into both categories warrant the greatest attention.

Here is another definition of dyslexia, from the Mayo Clinic:

Dyslexia is a learning disorder that involves difficulty reading due to problems identifying speech sounds and learning how they relate to letters and words (decoding). Also called reading disability, dyslexia affects areas of the brain that process language.[15]

Accommodations for Students with Dyslexia

Accommodations are assistances that allow a student to do the same work at the same level as other students such as:

- Extended time on tests
- Discounting of spelling on classwork
- Books on tape
- Text-to-speech devices/apps
- Spellcheck
- Copy of teachers' notes
- Peer note-taker
- Voice recognition software

Modifications for Students with Dyslexia

Modifications are changes in the academic style and demand on the students such as:

- Reduced number of assignments or items on an assignment
- Credit for oral work
- Reading lower-level books instead of grade-level books—also known as high-interest/low-skill-level books
- Clarification/simplification of written instruction

Reading instruction should directly include:

- Phonological Awareness
- Sound–Symbol Relations
- Multisensory Instruction
- Syllable Instruction
- Reading Comprehension Instruction
- Reading Fluency Instruction
- Morphology
- Syntax

The History of Dyslexia and ADHD

The histories of the conditions now known as dyslexia and ADHD are intertwined, and date back to the late 1800s. ADHD and dyslexia often get clumped together, but by outlining here their specific histories, we can see their distinctness. The timeline looks like this:

1877: The term "word blindness" first comes into use to describe individuals who do not have the ability to read or understand text accurately due to visual issues. (This theory of the cause of dyslexia was later rejected, after science identified PA.) Adolf Kussmaul, a German neurologist, describes how the power of sight, the intellect, and the ability to speak are all completely functional in people with dyslexia.

1905: W. E. Bruner first identifies reading problems in US children.

1930s: The term "dyslexia" is first used commonly in the United States.

1961: Ritalin is approved to treat ADHD, then called "hyperkinesis."

1963: Samuel Kirk first uses the term "learning disability" at an educational conference.

1968: The term "Hyperkinetic Reaction of Childhood" is adopted for use in the American Psychiatric Association's *Diagnostic and Statistical Manual of Mental Disorders* (DSM).

1969: Congress passes first law supporting children with learning disabilities.

1973: Congress passes Section 504 of the Rehabilitation Act which makes it illegal to discriminate against people with disabilities.

1975: Congress passes an act that requires all students to receive a free and appropriate education.

1980: The DSM renames ADHD as "Attention Deficit Disorder (with and without Hyperactivity)." According to Understood for All, "The DSM definition assumed that attention difficulties weren't related to impulsivity and hyperactivity. ADD was defined as a problem of inattention that could be accompanied by hyperactivity."[16]

1985: The first law supporting the rights of individuals with dyslexia was passed in Texas. This law required that all students be screened for dyslexia and provided with appropriate instruction.

1987: The DSM removed "ADD without hyperactivity" as a subtype of ADHD and decided to call every diagnosis ADHD with and without hyperactivity.

1990: Congress passes the Americans with Disabilities Act (ADA). This law stops discrimination against individuals with disabilities in both the workplace and public sector.

Why Should We Care?

What does it feel like to not fit in with our very left-brain society? It feels bad.

In fact, though, it's okay to be in your right brain—even better some-times. Like right handedness, our society tends to embrace those in their left brain (e.g., good organizational and ordering skill, good mechanical skills in reading, writing, and math) because they are predictable and consistent. We can understand how they work and process, like a robot. But, even though as a child it often doesn't feel good, it's quite an amazing thing to be in your right brain. That's where all the imagination, higher-level thinking, creativity, and mind-fulness live. These are such important skills which unfortunately—and right now particularly—our society does not value as much as those in the left brain.

> *I think 99 times and find nothing.*
> *I stop thinking, swim in silence,*
> *and the truth comes to me.*
> —Albert Einstein, *The Ultimate Quotable Einstein*

For anyone who cares about readers with dyslexia, this is a great time to be alive! Science and technology are advancing at a fast pace. Continued research is crucial, because a young child can get frustrated when learning to read—and this feeling of frustration around books and other text persists for a long time. It affects almost one in five chil-dren, which translates to ten million children in America alone.

The resulting lack of confidence pervades everything. Children with dyslexia are perplexed by phonology and words on a page, although they usually love listening to stories. Students with dyslexia often struggle with other skills in addition to reading such as spelling, artic-ulation, word retrieval, and fact recall. Both parents and teachers wonder whether they did something wrong. We know now why students with dyslexia struggle to read; it is a complex problem rooted in basic neurology and brain systems that relate to language.

Some children love to read and pick it up very easily. Often these children are called "linen closet kids" because they potentially could learn to read by reading the tags from the linens in the hall closet. Other children have a harder time. Even though these children are often very intelligent and creative, and love listening to stories read to them out loud, they struggle with phonological awareness and decoding (or sounding out phonetically) words. Often this difficulty with phonology exists within a circle of strengths such as critical thinking, creativity, logic, and the ability to make connections using higher-level cognition. For example, individuals with dyslexia can often understand and be deeply motivated to learn how a computer functions, enjoying the act of taking it apart and seeing how it all works together, though they will often struggle with spelling or even reading the word "cat." And I have known many students who could do advanced chemistry better than most, but who struggled to read anything fluently out loud.

The fact that we overemphasize phonology very early on, even in preschool, is extremely unfair, especially to the student with dyslexia.

> *We have to look, examine, investigate.*
> *We have to find what's really true,*
> *not just accept what someone else tells us.*
> —Sharon Salzberg, "The Issue of Faith in a
> Non-theistic Religion"

It is not always easy to diagnose dyslexia (and it is underdiagnosed by about 15%). There are several reasons for this including developmental variability, inconsistency, and unevenness. These are all described later in this chapter. Sometimes we underdiagnose, overdiagnose, or diagnose too early or too late. Either under- or overdiagnosing is bad for different reasons. If we underdiagnose, then we miss kids who can learn to read accurately and fast but don't—and their reading suffers.

If we overdiagnose, then we provide extra, invaluable services to those who do not need them, depleting resources to the detriment of those who do.

How Do We Know It's Dyslexia?

Dyslexia is also known as a language-based learning disability (LD), specific language disability, word blindness, or strephosymbolia. The Research Committee of the International Dyslexia Society defines dyslexia very similarly to the federal definition of LD (which is quoted in Chapters 4 and 5):

"Dyslexia is not only a visual processing or visual perceptual disorder in which the student sees letters, numbers and words in reverse, and mirror writes—it is a language deficiency with its roots in difficulties in phonological coding (sound–symbol relationships), isolating phonemes, syllable segmentation, vocabulary weaknesses, grammar and syntax confusion. Overall, it's a general deficiency in using language in any way to convey information."

To understand the complex assessment process by which a student is diagnosed with an LD, I have provided the full text of Mike's assessment, conducted by Dr. Julia Blodgett when he was 12 (see Appendix B). The assessment is extremely thorough and necessarily lengthy and serves as a model of how students with LDs should be assessed. Mike was diagnosed with multiple LDs, but the main one was dyslexia. He also proved to be exceptionally bright, so the report showed huge discrepancies between skills; Dr. Blodgett had not seen such a wide spread in a long time. Because of these discrepancies Mike was extremely frustrated, anxious, and angry. He needed special attention as well as accommodations and modifications (see Appendix B for the full report).

We knew something complicated was going on with Mike. Dr. Blodgett's assessment really helped to validate and clarify everything, and it provided some ideas for going forward with his tutoring.

Giving Children Special Help to Maintain Grade Level

Needless to say, Mike is not alone. Children throughout the United States and around the world struggle every day with LD, diagnosed or not.

Children are generally more likely to maintain their grade levels when special help is provided as early as first and second grade. Not providing special help until third grade—when schoolchildren in many states will take mandatory reading tests—often results in significantly lower success with grade-level reading.

It only gets worse thereafter, if interventions begin in fourth or fifth grade. As a report from the National Center for Learning Disabilities (NCLD) explains, "learning disabilities don't suddenly appear in third grade. Researchers have noted that the achievement gap between typical readers and those with dyslexia is evident as early as first grade. But many students struggle for years before they are identified with [specific learning disabilities] and receive needed support."[17]

In addition, research demonstrates that 66% of the children given special help are boys, and that people of color are overrepresented as having a learning disability in the school populations studied. Among high school students, between 12 and 26% with LD got average or above-average scores on math and reading assessments.

Another key finding, reinforcing the importance of continued improvement in both diagnosis and treatment, was that one third of LD students had been held back a grade in school.[18] The same NCLD report illustrates this dramatically. "Students with IEPs[19] were 85% more likely—and students with 504 plans[20] were 110% more likely—to repeat a grade than their peers without disabilities in 2013–2014. Retention [holding back a grade] increases the risk of dropping out."[21]

My primary takeaways:

- We do better with literacy when we intervene early.
- More individuals of color are identified for special ed than perhaps should be.

How Do We Teach These Children?

Hopefully this whole book will help the reader better understand the emotional, social, and academic needs of the individual with dyslexia. But for knowing how to deal with them in a classroom setting, this section will be helpful. Students with dyslexia, though charming, can be difficult behaviorally and academically. It is important for a teacher to think carefully about how they treat them in the classroom. Following are some tips. These tips can no doubt help all students, not just those with dyslexia.

Directly Teach One Concept at a Time.

Be careful not to multitask. Be mindful of everything you do and be very explicit. Be sure to task analyze whenever you can. This means breaking stuff down into small manageable chunks.

Make Sure That All Projects Are Relevant to Students' Lives.

Students with dyslexia are extremely discriminating when it comes to interest. That means they must see that the topic has some relevance to their lives. This is hard for a teacher to do at times, but it is very important. Students with dyslexia will shut down and appear stupid or lazy —when in fact they are neither—if the content is boring.

Teachers Must Give Students Acceptable Reasons to Wiggle and Move.

All students will benefit from being allowed to move around in the way that suits them. Some acceptable ways to move include having class jobs, holding or playing with class toys, taking care of the class pet, gesturing, stretching, frequent transitioning, and using standing work stations.

Keep the Rules in View and Refer to Them Often.

Many times, students with dyslexia will get in trouble for not following the rules, when, in fact, they simply cannot remember the rules, don't know them, or don't understand them. It behooves teachers to go over them on the first day of school, and then re-explain them, and refer to them often. It's great for all students to internalize them.

For students with dyslexia the difficulty lies in the storage and retrieval system (the processing of information) as it relates to language. The bottom line is that dyslexia is a problem with language, not with visual perception. Therefore, problems occur in the left side of the brain.

Although it is important to remember that every individual with dyslexia is unique and has different strengths and weaknesses, it is still possible to generalize somewhat as long as we are always careful not to overgeneralize. They often excel at "right-brained" tasks like math, art, or anything visual and spatial. They are often—not always—left-handed. They are often poor talkers before they are poor readers. They can wrongly appear as lazy or careless or stupid. Under stress the specific difficulties are exacerbated. They sometimes have strengths in auditory processing and memory and learn best this way, and sometimes visual processing is added in to that mix as a strength as well.

When these individuals can talk to someone (usually an adult) one-on-one or are allowed time to think through a complicated, often deep question, they shine. They can be shy in large groups, usually because they find these groups intimidating (don't we all?) and have lower self-esteem due to the language problems.

The parent of the individual with dyslexia is an amazing advocate. They often are very close to the individual and sometimes also can share the dyslexia and all its side effects, all of which make the parent an effective and loving support net. This parent undoubtedly wants the best for their child, but the parent is often not the best person to provide instruction or support. This is because a parent tends to be too close (hard to imagine, but if you've been a parent, you probably know what I mean). This means the parent may not be able to be objective, or may get frustrated because they may want their child to be magically "fixed" by what the parent can provide. Also, the parent may overly worry or compare their child to others, and thereby get upset.

Also, it can be helpful to have another unrelated person close because sometimes it can be hard for a young person to speak honestly with a parent (I get this, being the mother of three teenage girls). Sometimes a friend, teacher, or tutor can be a very strong advocate for the individual with dyslexia—as well as someone to lean on and trust with secrets. This can take tremendous pressure off parents and can offer the individual another positive relationship that expands the support net and allows the person with dyslexia to feel good about themself.

Another loving and supportive person who knows the individual well can be a sincere and effective advocate for that individual with dyslexia. Both the parents and the individual with dyslexia benefit because this person can provide objectivity as well as support, and for the parents this person can be a much-needed respite from grueling advocacy work that always needs to be done for the individual with dyslexia.

It's important to take the good days with the bad. Sometimes those with dyslexia can feel their brilliance and can shine. I call these "glass half-full" days. What can follow is a day fraught with problems and mistakes. I call these "glass half-empty" days. The good news is that we can learn tons from our "glass half-empty" days. Someone with dyslexia will benefit from starting each day positively, as a "glass half-full" day. If it turns to become negative, there will be ample opportunities for learning. Then there will be those truly horrible days, and no amount of positivity will help. Then we must ask, "Am I hungry? Thirsty? Tired? Do I need to isolate from others to avoid exploding at them?" Then it can be helpful to have and use this knowledge appropriately. This kind of self-monitoring is complex and can get deeply at self-esteem issues, which are hard to change without intensive effort.

3   MIKE'S EARLY YEARS

While we try to teach our children all about life,
Our children teach us what life is all about.
—Angela Schwindt

Regarding Mike's early years, he had a hard time meeting the milestones of infancy and toddlerhood. This was particularly pronounced because his older brother was precocious. Emily commented that when Mike was two and a half, he could understand language, but was slower to talk. At that time, she sensed that he might have a learning disability (LD). She noted many red flags, and her son reminded her of herself when she was younger. He was indeed pressured into spoken language by his sensitivity to loud sounds. His first sentence was "No more *Nessun Dorma!*" which referred to the opera Keith was blaring on the stereo. Emily and Keith stared at him, then clapped. Keith quickly turned the music down.

Also, Emily noticed that Mike did not have a dominant hand. Emily says,

---

He alternated which hand he used to hold a crayon, and even then, his grip was wrong. He also had a terrible time with hand-coordination. He couldn't make letters even though he knew what they were and what they should look like. We brought him to an occupational therapist for several years to help with his writing and hand-eye coordination. It was then he settled on the left hand for writing.

By four, he was significantly behind his peers in writing, spelling, drawing, and 'reading.' Learning how to spell his name was arduous so we gave up on the last name and just focused on 'Mike.' It wasn't until well into grade school that he could spell his last name. He loved listening to books but had a hard time manipulating them correctly. We'd often find him holding them backwards or upside down. His drawings appeared abstract although they were meant to be something particular. We got good at interpreting the squiggles. And often they were very sophisticated ideas.

He also was behind in picking up Spanish from his language immersion preschool. As with English, it was clear that he understood what was being said but never said anything in return. Nonetheless, he was a favorite with the teachers—bright, funny, and insightful beyond his years. It was so clear that there was a lot going on in his head but little ability to get it out.

These issues exacerbated Mike's inclination toward being alone. All the stimulation and hard work of learning exhausted him and he would crumble if not given a chance to be quiet and regroup. At the school, the teachers made him a quiet zone out of a blanket over a table. He was free to go under the table whenever he was overwhelmed, and then he would re-emerge 15–20 minutes later, ready to engage again. This pattern of lots going on in his brain, being exhausted, and needing some "down time" is common for students with dyslexia.

Mike was one of many students whom I taught to read, but he was at once my most gifted and most disabled student. I thought that my students were all amazing but unfairly treated.

4 WHAT IS LD AND WHERE DOES DYSLEXIA FIT IN?

Many times what we perceive as an error or failure
is actually a gift. And eventually we find that lessons
learned from that discouraging experience
prove to be of great worth.
—Richelle E. Goodrich, *Smile Anyway*

Over two million individuals in the United States have one or more learning disabilities (LDs) and 5–9% of school-aged students have an identified LD. Nine percent of students with LD drop out of school and 20% of high schoolers with LD are five or more years behind in reading. Sixty percent of students with LD have poor reading skills at the beginning of high school (if their disability was not identified by second grade).

Federal Definition

Specific learning disability means a disorder in one or more of the basic psychological processes involved in understanding or in using language, spoken or written, that may manifest itself in the imperfect ability to listen, think, speak, read, write, spell, or to do mathematical calculations, including conditions such as perceptual disabilities, brain injury, minimal brain dysfunction, dyslexia, and developmental aphasia. . . . Specific learning disability does not include learning problems that are primarily the result of visual, hearing, or motor disabilities, of intellectual disability, of emotional disturbance, or of environmental, cultural, or economic disadvantage.[1]

Comments about Learning Disabilities

Children with LD share some disorder or some brain dysfunction that delays the learning process. This can play out in many different ways.

1. LD is a big umbrella that arches over many different types of learning issues.
2. LD is a manmade construct and thus can vary by definition from state to state (in other words, you can be defined as LD in one state but not another) whereas dyslexia does not vary because it is neurologic, not manmade.
3. Children with LD can have problems with some or all of these skills: listening, thinking, talking, reading, writing, spelling, doing math.
4. These problems are not the result of vision or hearing problems, physical handicaps, emotional problems, or an emotionally traumatic event such as divorce, economic, or

cultural disadvantage—**although teachers may make similar accommodations in their classroom for such children.**

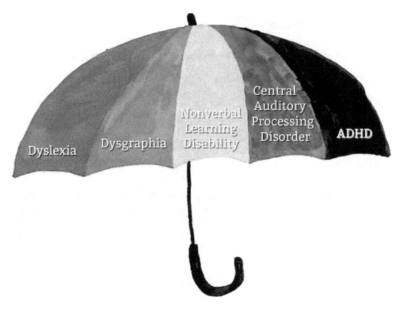

The conditions under the LD umbrella: Dyslexia, Dysgraphia, Nonverbal Learning Disability, Central Auditory Processing Disorder, and ADHD

Knowing yourself
is the beginning of all wisdom.
—Aristotle

Learning Disability

Dyslexia is one of a number of different LDs. When we test for an LD, the defining characteristics we look for are the skill levels of each individual.

Don't be fooled by unevenness or inconsistency. With LD there are incredible strengths as well as weaknesses, and incredible compensatory strategies. The "one day they can do it and the next they can't"

phenomenon is a good example of this (the best example is the child with attention-deficit hyperactivity disorder [ADHD] in front of a computer). Test scores fluctuate immensely as a result.

Developmental Issues around LD

Many of the signs of LD are behaviors that are developmentally appropriate at certain ages (specifically speech issues and handwriting). For example, speech transpositions like "sawabi" for "wasabi," or mirror writing (reversals in which the letters are backwards) tend to appear from age 4 to age 7. **Therefore, early identification of LD is controversial.**

Educators are divided as to the use of early testing (before second and third grade) for LD. Some prefer to wait and see, respecting variability through second and third grade, while others emphasize the importance of testing children early for possible LD. I think we can do both, meaning we can both respect variability while still being tuned in to "red flags" that may indicate an LD. This way, if a student has some "red flags," they should be tested at the beginning of second grade, with intervention beginning by the middle or end of second grade, if necessary.

Dysgraphia

Dysgraphia is also known as motor agraphia and is described by a loss of the ability to express ideas in writing because of problems with motor production. The motor component interferes with expression. Handwriting is difficult to read and very labored. Unless it is found comorbid with dyslexia, which is common, dysgraphia exists in the presence of strong reading and spelling skills (children understand what they read and write—it's the actual act of writing that is hard for them). Boys and left-handed students are more likely to be affected.

Nonverbal Learning Disability (NLD)

Students with NLD have excellent verbal skills, and are good at reading, spelling, and writing. NLD means there is some kind of glitch or LD in nonverbal processing. Unlike dyslexia, NLDs are neurological syndromes resulting from damage to the right side of the brain. Three categories of dysfunction present themselves:

1. Motor problems (lack of coordination, balance problems, difficulty with fine motor skills)
2. Visual-spatial-organizational skill deficits
3. Social skill deficits (poor social judgment, difficulty in novel situations, difficulty reading social cues)

These students with NLD also have strong auditory attention. They learn best through verbal channels, which they use to compensate for weaknesses. They have strong memory, learn rote material easily, and view things in a step-by-step manner. They have trouble with seeing the whole, big picture (part-to-whole relationships are tricky [e.g., fractions]), and do better with sequential processing as opposed to simultaneous processing. Basically, NLD is the exact opposite of dyslexia and looks a lot like ADHD because the difficulty is in attending to visual and tactile input. HOWEVER, not all children with NLD talk and read early—sometimes they have trouble with the initial stages of reading, and can be misdiagnosed with dyslexia.

Central Auditory Processing Disorder (CAPD)

CAPD is also known as aphasia, anomia, or receptive language disorder. It occurs when a child has the ability to hear but is unable to process and take meaning from the language they hear surrounding them. As a result, this child has a hard time establishing rapport with adults. It can be very hard to spot because it is receptive which means it affects their understanding as opposed to expressing language, and thus isn't always apparent to an onlooker. Kids can usually reach age 5 or 6 before it is noticed, and their condition can look like other things like ADHD or a behavior disorder.

For children with CAPD, movement is toward solitary play or play with other kids where action is more important than words. Following directions is very difficult, especially multistep directions. Once kids hit elementary school, following directions is vital to success. These students usually look to other kids, watch what they do in response to a direction, and then follow their lead. If given a direction alone, those with CAPD will respond with a smile or a nod and then not comply. Adults find this frustrating, and think it is an attention or defiant behavior problem.

Most children also have expressive language problems since the two are dependent on each other. For this reason, writing and spelling mistakes can be a sign of a problem (e.g., "I ate pancakes the smorning") and these students also show large gaps in many areas. Priscilla Vail claims that spoonerisms and malapropisms are good diagnostic tools (Rittle Lead Hen, BiteLear for Buzz Light Year, skin milk, or "take the ball by the horns").

To summarize, CAPD is complex, and often hard to diagnose because it can look like many other differences. It is also confusing because it can take many different forms, looking very different for each student.

ADHD

ADHD is neurobehavioral in nature and affects both adults and children. It often is described as severe inattention, impulsivity, and at times, hyperactivity. ADHD is often treated behaviorally as well as medically. Results of these treatments are mixed, and are dependent on the individual. Often individuals with ADHD have difficulty with time management, organization, and paying attention to what is being said.

Summary of the Types of Learning Disabilities

As our multi-toned umbrella showed us, there are many types of LDs. Here I've included a popular but not exhaustive list of some types. These include dyslexia, dysgraphia, NLD, CAPD, and ADHD. These can all be tricky because they often coexist—or don't—and often look alike. It is important to try to tease them apart and that is why a perceptive and thorough assessment is critical and not to be taken lightly.

Summarizing Comments about Learning Disabilities

1. Children with LD share some disorder / some brain dysfunction that delays the learning process. This can play out in many different ways.
2. LD is a big umbrella that arches over many different types of learning issues.
3. Dyslexia is under that big umbrella.
4. Students with LD can have problems with listening, thinking, talking, reading, writing, spelling, and doing math.
5. These are not the result of vision or hearing problems, physical handicaps, emotional problems, or an emotionally traumatic event such as divorce, economic, or cultural disadvantage **—although you may make similar accommodations in those individuals.**
6. When we **test** for an LD, the main things we look for are skills deficits.
7. **Don't be fooled by unevenness.** Students with LD possess

incredible strengths as well as weaknesses, and demonstrate impressive compensatory strategies.

8. **Don't be fooled by inconsistency** (e.g., one day they can do it and the next they can't). The best example is the child with ADHD in front of the computer.

9. **Developmental issues around LD**. Many of the signs of LD show up as variations in behaviors that are developmentally appropriate at certain ages.

Developmental Variability

Children all progress at different rates. This makes it hard to diagnose dyslexia at a young age, even though it is of utmost importance. Now it seems to make the most sense to diagnose dyslexia no later than mid-second grade. (We also need to consider the many red flags like familial dyslexia, handedness, and problems across contexts, all of which should be taken only as red flags, not as diagnostic of dyslexia.) Any earlier and we may mistake developmental variability for dyslexia, which would be tragic for the child. Any later and the problems of dyslexia become rooted and part of the child's identity, which is not how it should be.

That is the biggest problem: when students with dyslexia feel that they are not as good or as smart as their peers, when in fact they are usually smarter. And this can pervade every area of their life, even those areas they are good at, whether it be sports, computer science, or theater. This is why it's important to address the inequities: when a talented or gifted child feels they are stupid or inadequate in some way, something is very wrong.

Warning Signs or "Red Flags" That Your Child May Need to Be Tested for Dyslexia

0–3 years

Struggling and significant delays in developmental milestones (crawling, walking, talking) is the first red flag for dyslexia. More specifically, some of the red flags include:

- Significant delays in language development
- Chronic ear infections (Remember, these are all red flags. Individually, they may mean nothing. It is important to consider the entire picture.)
- Family history of dyslexia
- Family history of left-handedness or ambidexterity

Preschool

In preschool, dyslexia becomes more apparent. This is because phonology, along with the printed word, becomes much more relevant and common than before formal schooling, especially now, when some three-year-olds are reading at advanced levels. Letters and words start to become important, so the student with dyslexia already begins to feel inadequate. The child or the parents often think there might be a problem, when it is still too early to tell. Nonetheless, it's helpful to be aware of some red flags or patterns that indicate there might be a problem. In addition to the previous bulleted list, these include:

- Trouble learning the alphabet
- Trouble with rhyming
- Trouble learning numbers, colors, days of the week, and shapes
- Inability to order events in a logical time frame by age 4— temporal sequencing

- Short attention span
- Delayed motor skills / physical clumsiness
- Difficulty with other children / peer interactions
- Continued delays in language development
- Not forming sentences or talking at all by age 3
- Word-finding problems
- Pronunciation problems

Grades 1–4

Some of the same problems of preschool occur while new ones also arise in these grades. It is important to keep vigilantly watching for red flags, specifically:

- Frequent frustration
- Trouble with reading
- Continued difficulty with phonemic awareness (sound–symbol relationships)
- Trouble developing a sight vocabulary (words recognized by sight)
- Consistent reading / spelling errors (reversals, inversions, transpositions, substitutions)

> *The light burning within you is a far more accurate*
> *reflection of who you are than the stories you've*
> *been telling yourself.*
> —B Grace Bullock, "Is Santosha
> (Contentment) Really Possible?"

The first two of the following red flags might seem like "green flags" to the layperson. However, high or advanced reasoning, and advanced conceptual understanding, within a context of other red flags, will create a striking kind of discrepancy. For example, high reasoning along with ear infections, dyslexia running in the family, and, most importantly, trouble with PA, as evidenced by poor reading fluency, etc., can help the alert parent seek a professional evaluation for their child.

Circle of Strengths

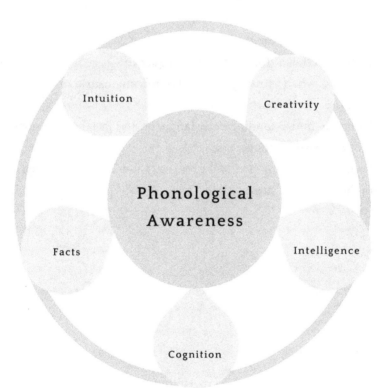

- High or advanced reasoning (parents start to see the circle of strengths around one overemphasized skill: PA). See Circle of Strengths diagram, above.
- Advanced conceptual understanding (parents start to see the universe of strengths).
- Trouble with math skills
- Trouble learning numbers and counting
- Math facts—slow recall
- Transposition of number sequences
- Confusion of arithmetic signs
- Inability to tell a story in a logical sequence
- Slowness when learning new skills—relying instead on memory
- Difficulty understanding body language and facial expressions
- Trouble learning about time
- Poor coordination—accident proneness and lack of awareness of their physical surrounding

5 TEACHING MIKE HOW TO READ

You cannot swim for new horizons until you have
courage to lose sight of the shore.
—William Faulkner, *The Mansion*

In Mike's second-grade year at school, I got a call from his mom, and began tutoring him. We worked together on how to read.

When we first began tutoring, Mike told me he wanted to be a photographer. When I asked him why, he said it was because photographers don't have to read anything. I knew then that we had a good deal of work to do in order to keep all doors open. I used the Orton-Gillingham approach, which I modified to make more interesting. According to Emily,

---

The one big step forward, dyslexia-wise was that I had him tested by the County Special Ed program and got him an IEP [Individualized

Education Program]. This was huge because it defined the challenge he had as well as his intelligence. It also required the school to take Mike's dyslexia seriously and acknowledge that the memorization-based reading/spelling methodology the school was using was not going to be successful—even if Mike worked harder. That insight brought some change to how he was being taught and some appreciation for his strengths. For him, the school moved away from memorization and more toward the Wilson method. The actual Wilson method was not used until fourth grade, but it was there as a reference for the teachers before that. The other helpful thing was the accommodations that the school now had to give Mike: double time on tests and other assessments; no points off for poor spelling on assignments; use of computers and other electronic devices; the ability to have a tutor (you!) come on campus and work with him at the end of the day; and, a revised workload in some situations. (Those are the ones that come to mind.)

What Is Dyslexia? Depends on Who You Ask!

What is dyslexia, and how is it different from other LDs? The answers can be confusing. Note that, while it's considered an LD, dyslexia is nuanced and is often not recognized by public schools.

> *We are all wonderful, beautiful wrecks.*
> *That's what connects us—*
> *that we're all broken,*
> *all beautifully imperfect.*
> —Emilio Estevez

Public schools generally do not diagnose dyslexia; they only diagnose "general LD," mostly for the purpose of writing the goals on the IEP. If a child does not qualify for the diagnosis of LD as the school defines it, the parents may hire and pay a private psychologist to diagnose dyslexia, which may be diagnosed even if LD is not, because LD, unlike dyslexia, is a manmade construct. As a practical matter, LD is a big umbrella used by the public schools to diagnose (or not) a child for "special education" services. Then it's on to the special ed teacher, who gets to know the child and refines the diagnosis to one of the umbrella terms (see p. 31).

Although a good public school teacher will see dyslexia in a child, it often falls to the family to bring in a private assessor to diagnose "dyslexia."

A student who is tested (privately) and given the identification of dyslexia, often has high intelligence and significantly lower achievement, making it difficult to access the grade–level curriculum. In contrast, a student who is tested (usually in public school) and given the identification of LD often shows a skill difference, with or without high intelligence, that interferes with their ability to learn, and/or access the curriculum.

As a consequence of this customary blanket use of "LD," each state can define LD in their own distinct way, and a child may be described as learning disabled in one state but not in another. This is both confusing and detrimental to the child.

For this reason and to reiterate (see p. 30), the federal government has stepped in with its overarching definition:

Specific learning disability means a disorder in one or more of the basic psychological processes involved in understanding or in using language, spoken or written, that may manifest itself in the imperfect ability to listen, think, speak, read, write, spell, or to do mathematical calculations, including conditions such as perceptual disabilities, brain injury, minimal brain dysfunction, dyslexia, and developmental aphasia. ... Specific learning disability does not include learning problems that are

primarily the result of visual, hearing, or motor disabilities, of intellectual
disability, of emotional disturbance, or of environmental, cultural, or
economic disadvantage.[1]

It is both interesting and understandable to me that all of the definitions presented here take a deficit approach. I do understand that these definitions must unpack how this child is different, what they lack, and why they need qualitatively different instruction. But I think we must also be very careful not to pigeonhole or track these students—due to weaknesses in reading and writing mechanics—if they have other strengths. It is important to look at all aspects of an individual and see the whole picture; the strengths along with the weaknesses.

6 HOW TO RETEACH READING

The privilege of a lifetime is being who you are.
—Joseph Campbell, *Joseph Campbell Companion*

It is critical that the teacher or tutor develop a sincere and close relationship with the individual with dyslexia first, in order to establish trust, which ultimately can lead to success. Teaching a person how to read, especially if dyslexia is an issue, involves much more than following the steps of an Orton-Gillingham (OG) program (as listed below). Those steps are necessary but not sufficient. The teacher or tutor must bring him or herself into the room and be willing to be honest and real with the student. This will allow a special relationship to develop, and it's important to always remember that there is no set amount of time that it will take. It is important not to rush this relationship. The combination of the OG approach with a close relationship between the student and teacher/tutor makes for a successful experience.

Reading Fluency

Great Leaps is the reading fluency program that I have used success-fully with my students with dyslexia.[1] Fluency is the ability to read smoothly, accurately, and with expression.[2] The less fluent or dysfluent reader must focus primarily on the mechanics of reading, leaving little room for comprehension or meaning. By contrast, the more fluent reader can focus less on the actual act of reading, leaving more energy for comprehension and the underlying message. Dysfluent readers usually have inconsistent speed, poor phrasing, and inadequate recog-nition of patterns, and they often ignore punctuation. According to NAEP's study of fourth graders, 49% of children read too slowly, and 43% read inaccurately and these are the students who could benefit from fluency training, specifically Great Leaps. This is important because fluency directly relates to comprehension. The bottom line is, "children who become fluent readers also make important gains in the ability to understand what they read."[3]

Order of Teaching Reading

There are many wonderful OG-based programs that individuals with dyslexia will respond to IF they have all the key components. To review, these include:

1. Phonological tools
2. Multisensory tools
3. Structured approach
4. Systematic approach
5. Sequential approach

FUN-R (Foundation Underlying New Reading)

Most programs that exist now are quite dry and have trouble main-taining the attention of the student. My literacy program, however, has more bells and whistles, more transitions, and is very engaging for students.

Each student selects and personalizes a special shared FUN-R note-book—usually a composition book or spiral notebook—in which the student and teacher/tutor collaborate. It is the student's book, so they put their name on the front, add stickers, and decorate it however they want. The student uses the notebook during tutoring. After the lesson, the teacher/tutor retains it until the next lesson. This assures the note-book doesn't get lost, and gives the teacher/tutor time to add to the notebook between lessons. So, for example, before teaching step 3 in the sequence that follows, the teacher/tutor will handwrite into the FUN-R notebook the specific rule—what all closed syllables need—to be addressed in the "Teach the Rule" portion of the lesson.

The FUN-R program follows the following sequence (bells and whis-tles not included):

1. Short vowels—Start Great Leaps Reading Fluency Programs—Pictures and short vowel sounds

- Teach order for flash cards (letter/object/sound)
- Read WII (Words In Isolation) for each short vowel (*grab, big, spend, clock, nut*)
- Do sandpaper letters
- Read sentences and phrases with short vowels
- Draw a picture of a sentence with short vowels

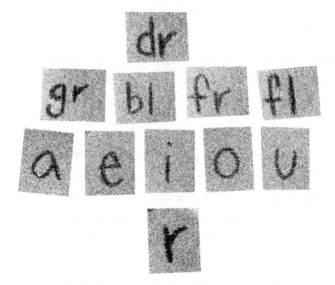

Examples of sandpaper letters and consonant blends, for
students to trace with their fingers and combine into words.

2. Consonant blends and digraph—Do Great Leaps exercises first and
last, to bookend every lesson

- Teach order for flash cards (letter / object / sound)
- Read WII (Words In Isolation) for each blend and digraph
  (*blend, clap, flex, frog, brim, trap, chin, shot, moth, phantom, when*)
- Do sandpaper letters
- Read sentences and phrases with blends and digraphs and
  draw a picture (*Fred bragged about jumping off a cliff into a trench
  and landed on a frog*)

3. Teach the 1st of 7 Syllables—CLOSED—Discriminate from OPEN—
Do Great Leaps exercises first and last, to bookend every lesson

- Teach the Rule—see FUN-R notebook for what all closed
  syllables need

- Read WII (Words In Isolation) for the CLOSED syllable (*grab, big, sped, clot, nut*)
- Do sandpaper words
- Read sentences and phrases with closed syllables
- Draw a picture of a sentence with closed syllables (*That red dog has the name Clifford*)

4. Teach the 2ⁿᵈ of 7 Syllables—OPEN—Do Great Leaps exercises first and last, to bookend every lesson

- Teach the Rule—see FUN-R notebook for what all open syllables need
- Read WII (Words In Isolation) for the OPEN syllable (*go, bi, me, a, nu*)
- Do sandpaper words
- Read sentences and phrases with open syllables
- Draw a picture of a sentence with open syllables (*Jojo likes to go fast on the wagon*)
- Play games with CLOSED and OPEN syllable types.
- Read WII (Words In Isolation) for the OPEN Syllable

5. Teach the 3rd of 7 Syllables—MAGICAL E Syllable—Do Great Leaps exercises first and last, to bookend every lesson

- Review the previous two syllable types
- Teach the Rule—see FUN-R notebook for what all MAGICAL E syllables need
- Read WII (Words In Isolation) for the MAGICAL E syllable (*time, ripe, pine*)
- Do MAGICAL E circle
- Do sandpaper words
- Read sentences and phrases with MAGICAL E syllables

- Draw a picture of a sentence with MAGICAL E syllables (*The mime likes to tame the snake*)
- Play games with CLOSED and OPEN and MAGICAL E syllable types.

6. Teach the 4th of 7 Syllables—POWER of R Syllable—Do Great Leaps exercises first and last, to bookend every lesson

- Review previous three syllable types
- Teach the Rule—see FUN-R notebook for what all POWER of R syllables need
- Read WII (Words In Isolation) for the POWER of R syllable (*star, hammer, corn, first, burn*)
- Do sandpaper words
- Read sentences and phrases with POWER of R syllable
- Draw a picture of a sentence with POWER of R syllables (*The hammer was firm and sharp but the gopher was furry and smart*)
- Play games with CLOSED, OPEN, MAGICAL E, and POWER of R syllable types.

7. Teach 1st of 4 Dividing Rules—DIVIDE BETWEEN TWO CONSO-NANTS—Do Great Leaps exercises first and last, to bookend the lesson

- Do worksheet called "DIVIDE BETWEEN TWO CONSONANTS—YES or NO?"
- Do WII
- Make up sentence and write and read it.
- Play boardgame with DIVIDE BETWEEN TWO CONSONANTS words

8. Teach 2nd and 3rd of 4 Dividing Rules—DIVIDE IN FRONT or IN BACK of One Consonant—Do Great Leaps exercises first and last, to bookend every lesson

- Do worksheet called, "DIVIDE IN FRONT or IN BACK of One Consonant—YES or NO?"
- Do WII
- Make up sentence and write and read it.
- Play boardgame with DIVIDE IN FRONT or IN BACK OF ONE CONSONANT words

9. Teach 5th of 7 Syllable Types—VOWEL TEAM—Do Great Leaps exercises first and last, to bookend every lesson

- Review previous four syllable types
- Teach the Rule—see FUN-R notebook for what all VOWEL TEAM syllables need
- Read WII (Words In Isolation) for the VOWEL TEAM Syllable (*read, coin, bow, boast, etc.*)
- Do sandpaper words
- Read sentences and phrases with VOWEL TEAM syllables
- Draw a picture of a sentence with VOWEL TEAM syllables (*The mime likes to tame the snake*)
- Play games with CLOSED, OPEN, MAGICAL E, POWER of R, and VOWEL TEAM syllable types

10. Teach 4th Dividing Rule—DIVIDE BETWEEN TWO VOWELS—Do Great Leaps exercises first and last, to bookend every lesson

- Do worksheet about dividing between two vowels
- Teach the Rule—see FUN-R notebook for how all words in which 2 VOWELS are DIVIDED behave
- Read WII (Words In Isolation) for the 4th dividing rule (*lion, create, violin, poem*)
- Do sandpaper words

- Read sentences and phrases with DIVIDE BETWEEN TWO VOWELS words
- Draw a picture of a sentence with DIVIDE BETWEEN TWO VOWEL words (*The lion created a very beautiful poem*)

11. Teach 6th of 7 Syllable Types—Cle Syllable—Do Great Leaps exercises first and last, to bookend every lesson

- Teach the Rule—see FUN-R notebook for what all Cle syllables need
- Read WII (Words In Isolation) for the Cle Syllable (*bubble, cradle, grapple, tackle*)
- Do sandpaper words
- Read sentences and phrases with Cle syllable
- Draw a picture of a sentence with Cle syllables (*It is hard to grapple with a bubble that will not pop*)

12. Teach hard and soft "c" and "g"

- Teach the Rule—see FUN-R notebook for what all soft c and g words need
- Read WII (Words In Isolation) for soft c and g words (*cement centipede, cellophane, gym, giraffe, giant*)
- Do sandpaper words
- Read sentences and phrases with soft c and g words.
- Draw a picture of a sentence with soft c and g words (*The giraffe was giant and soft but the centipede was hard as cement.*)

13. Teach Affixes—Prefixes and Suffixes

- Teach nonsense syllables
- Teach the Rule—see FUN-R notebook for what all Affixes need

- Read WII (Words In Isolation) for the Affixes (*construction, prediction, substitute*)
- Do sandpaper words
- Read sentences and phrases with Affixes
- Draw a picture of a sentence with Affixes (*Be careful of the construction and the madness of the transportation*)

14. Teach Spelling /k/

- Teach the Rule—see FUN-R notebook for what all Spelling /k/ words have
- Read WII (Words In Isolation) for the Spelling of /k/ (*cracked, truck, like*)
- Do sandpaper words
- Read sentences and phrases with /k/ spellings
- Draw a picture of a sentence with spelling /k/ words (*The electric truck sank in the lake*)

Summary of How to Teach Reading

The main components for good reading instruction include an approach that follows the OG philosophy, a good fluency program with immediate rewards, and a good relationship between the teacher and student (all of those are included here).[4] However, this recipe is not as easy as it looks. Each lesson should be catered to each individual student, with the proportions of each critical component tailored to the student's needs. I cannot reiterate too much how important a sincere and comfortable relationship is between the student and teacher. It can make or break success for that student.

7 MIKE AND WRITING

At times, our own light goes out and is rekindled by a spark from another person. Each of us has cause to think with deep gratitude of those who have lighted the flame within us.
— Albert Schweitzer

Mike

May 1 (2017)

It was a great help to me when I was finally told the name of what I was suffering from, dyslexia, the miasma of uncertainty about my abilities as a student had been greatly crippled just in learning that what I had was a known problem that others suffered from, the unease that filled my mind crumbled more as my parents told me more about Dyslexia and the strengths and weakness associated with it. In the span of a few weeks what was once an unknowable force that I could do nothing about became a known variable that I could affect and as I could affect it I knew that i could beat it.

I began teaching Mike writing in middle school, which for Mike was fifth grade. I began by teaching the organization of a paragraph using the analogy of a burrito, with the main idea being the main ingredient such as the meat or the beans, and the detail sentences being all the juicy fixin's.

For the writing portion of Mike's tutorial, I chose to use two methods: one that I created, called "A Paragraph Is Like a Burrito" and another larger, more stylistic approach by Ruth Culham called *6 + 1 Traits of Writing.*[1]

During my first six writing tutorial sessions with Mike, we worked on paragraph development and organization, specifically identifying and writing the main idea sentence, the detail sentences, and the closing sentence. As Mike's tutor, I explained it this way:

"A really good paragraph that you read or write has inside of it lots of juicy and tasty details that fill you up. The part of a burrito that holds everything together is the tortilla. You can't have a good burrito without a solid tortilla, the main ingredient like meat or beans (the Main Idea) and all the juicy and delicious fixin's (the details) such as lettuce, cheese, guacamole, tomatoes, and rice. That's what makes the burrito taste so good and makes one burrito taste different from another burrito. The fixin's give the burrito flavor and personality. So when you write a paragraph, you must remember all the parts of a burrito, and include them all so as to make your paragraph meaningful and organized but also interesting and riveting (make sure you have a Main Idea Sentence that everything else is about and Detail Sentences that are tasty, delicious, and inviting)."

I recognized that Mike struggles with getting his ideas from his head to his oral expression and then to written expression. In other words, every step of the way there is a glitch. Even though Mike was so talkative with me, his tutor, things changed dramatically both in quality and quantity when he thought about the formal process of putting something into writing, though I knew the material was inside of him. When we're just talking, Mike can stream through many interesting facts and be funny and fluid. When I put the graphic organizer (see illustration, below) in front of him, and talk about putting thoughts on paper, Mike automatically becomes stilted, even when I stress that we are just jotting down thoughts, not full sentences, and even when I say I will write it for him. Because I wanted Mike to become more masterful at thinking fluidly and in an organized way and to be able to articulate clearly, we originally did a lot of brainstorming and paragraph organization before actually writing, with verbal expression of the final paragraph. Before actually writing anything, I gave Mike a writing pep talk.

"Writing is hard! Anyone your age—or any age—thinks this because it is true. Writing is the most complex task your brain can engage in. What's so hard about it? Anyone can write, but writing well is how it gets tricky. Well, the organizational aspects are hard, to start. We have all these thoughts in our head, and when we write we have to figure out how to order them as well as figure out how much detail to include and what words to use, not to mention grammar and spelling. Ugh! You may feel overwhelmed and that you can't do it. But you can! And well! If you have dyslexia, the organizational parts are even harder, because you are asking your brain to do those organizational tasks—like spelling, word choosing, and getting thoughts on paper—that your brain is not wired to do, and therefore is no good at. Also, if you have dyslexia —and here's the tricky part—you may become even more frustrated with writing, because often with dyslexia—not always, but often and definitely with you, Mike—there is strength in imagination, intuition, creativity, and cognitive connecting, so the ideas flow but the mechanics and organization do not. There is such a great discrepancy between these two constructs that the frustration can get to be overwhelming and stifling. Typing as opposed to handwriting definitely can help. But it is another learning curve to go up. Once typing is mastered, we can move on to more writing. So, what should we do? PRACTICE the writing!"

I used graphic organizers for breaking down both reading and writing. Mike would read a book and when I asked some questions, he would complete a graphic organizer with the main idea of the book or chapter in the middle and the details all around it, organized in layers and sublayers (or bubbles and sub-bubbles). We would do the same for writing except Mike would come up with ideas in his head and we would use a graphic organizer to keep them organized and out of his head and onto paper. One summer, Mike wrote a book, with my help. He used this kind of tool to organize his thoughts into chapters, paragraphs, and ultimately the whole trajectory of the story.

2/28

The kids thought Miss Daisy was an impostor. The kids talked about it in the cafeteria during lunch.

Miss Daisy did not know how to read or write or do arithmetic. They decided they were not going to tell anyone. They did not want to learn anything and just wanted to have fun. Who do you think Miss Daisy really is?

Source text for the student's use with graphic organizer

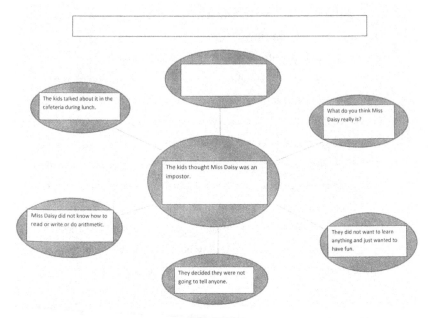

The "Miss Daisy" source text as parsed out with an example of a graphic
organizer

The student with dyslexia must work harder and write more. It seems
so unfair, but I have had students who have come to love writing and
who have turned to it as an outlet. Mike and I did spend a good part of
the year brainstorming and typing, before getting to the actual writing.
But it was certainly worth it. We covered different kinds of paragraphs,
such as descriptive, debate, character description, and sequential order.
We also talked about and practiced editing, using the COPS mnemonic
(Capitalization, Order, Punctuation, and Spelling) as well as enhancing
word choice, to make the writing come alive and make the paragraph
details juicier, like fixin's on a burrito. Mike did really well, and is a
phenomenal writer due to a combination of creativity—which comes
from natural ability—and a strong appetite for reading. We continued
to work on typing, organization, and continually trying to go around

the glitches among the cognitive, oral, and written pathways in his brain, for which there are no easy or quick solutions, unfortunately. Corresponding with Mike's dad Keith, I wrote,

---

"Mike has made great progress, but it often doesn't show during our planned sessions. In my attempts to stay positive, I try to honor his feelings while still getting at the objective of the lesson. I almost always do, either by reconfiguring the order of the lesson, or throwing in some reading (which is almost always good for writing, through modeling and recognizing methods of voice, organization and sentence fluency, within what we read, giving both good and bad examples). Mike openly expresses objections to what I have planned.

"I also do believe the keyboarding is critical for Mike. Typing, once mastered, will be quite freeing for Mike, given his issues with handwriting.

"Mike responds well to positive reinforcement. He needs to know that he is really good at writing! He's great at creative expression through word choice, voice, idea formation, and sentence fluency. BUT he gets blocked by the mechanics, the conventions, and the COPS (Capitalization, Order, Punctuation and Spelling). This is why his knee-jerk reaction to writing is usually "no." But I can almost always find a way around it and get some good writing out of him. He craves more structure than not, most of the time. He struggles with spelling, longer assignments, and punctuation and these inhibit his natural gift of writing. He needs support and positive reinforcement to get his ideas down on paper. We have begun editing, a crucial part of writing for Mike, as well as for everyone.

Mike's poetry is beautiful! He has a great sense of melody with his sentences. It comes from within but only sometimes. He needs to be inspired and engaged, and needs to have all the anxiety removed from his brain, so that the creativity can come out. Anxiety and lack of confidence are two huge blocks to written expression."

---

8 HOW TO RETEACH WRITING

Dripping water hollows out stone,
not through force but through persistence.
—Ovid

Mike is an exceptional writer and is extremely smart, so I was able to use a pretty advanced text with him and let him figure out how to get around his mechanical glitches. I was eager to stay out of his way and not sabotage his creativity. This is unusual and unlike most students with dyslexia, for whom I would provide more structure.

For most students with dyslexia, I would reteach writing in the following way:

Lots of Dictating

With this approach, the tutor writes down what the student says. I love this technique! It is a great way to start because it eliminates any fear a student may have about writing mechanics. It allows the students space to soar with their ideas unencumbered by all of the mechanical glitches they may have.

Lots of Brainstorming Ideas

With this approach, the tutor continues to write down whatever the student comes up with when brainstorming ideas for paragraphs and stories. This happens early in the writing process so that students can think freely and invent their most creative ideas without having to worry about the mechanics.

When They Can't Write

This is a text by Charlotte Morgan for mechanics and different styles of writing.[1] I like this approach for students with dyslexia because it is multisensory, structured, sequential, and interactive, which enables students to access the material easily and successfully.

Mavis Beacon to Reteach Typing

The Mavis Beacon Teaches Typing program will teach typing to mastery. I would also recommend using fun typing games on the internet. These can be highly motivating for all students, but particularly those with dyslexia or attention-deficit hyperactivity disorder (ADHD). When students master typing, they often show incredible progress with their writing. Though typing mastery is often not easy to attain, it can be well worth it in the end.

> *Start where you are*
> *Use what you have*
> *Do what you can.*
> —Arthur Ashe

Every Student Is Unique and Should Be Taught that Way

Writing is a hard skill to acquire, as well as to teach. Some students with dyslexia and ADHD can be really good at it, while others can be really bad at it.

Here are some of my key points for teachers, parents, and helping professionals when it comes to introducing students with dyslexia and ADHD to writing.

- Be very careful about making assumptions about your students.
- Meet each one where they are; you as a teacher, parent, or professional may be pleasantly surprised.
- Always remember that one size never fits all, and often fits nobody.
- Students are all special and unique and should be treated as such.
- When it comes to writing, never forget that for some students the mechanics like spelling, punctuation, capital letters, or organization may be the weakest link. For others, idea formation, brainstorming, or comprehension may be weak.
- Always remember that each student is different in every way, and must be respected individually, in order to do their best work.

Building Rapport—Good for Writing and Every Other Subject, Too

Students with dyslexia need to hear frequently that they are worthy of love. They need to hear that they are lovable from parents, teachers, and peers, and anyone else who spends time with them. They need to know that people like to spend time with them. Probably the most important thing adults can do when interacting with students with dyslexia is to uplift not only their own dignity but that of the students' as well.

I advise a focus on calling the student by name, finding the good in them, and highlighting all the strengths that the student has, pointing them out as much as possible. Overlook, if you can, the students' weaknesses or problems. Be tolerant and use a sense of humor whenever interacting with the student.

Always remember that preparation and creativity in lesson planning can prevent classroom behavior problems. Also, remember to give specific and clear instructions to students so that they will maintain confidence.

9 MIKE AND MATH

Quiet the mind and the soul will speak.
—Ma Jaya Sati Bhagavati, *The 11 Karmic Spaces*

I worked with Mike on math in middle school. At that time, he was showing the ways in which PA (phonological awareness) was affecting his reading and writing in school. Now it was obvious to me that PA was also affecting Mike's mathematics performance. He often got mixed up when reading signs (e.g., +, -, x), had great difficulty memorizing number facts, or understanding clocks and money, and he would often reverse and transpose numbers. He also would mix up the four quadrants, so graphing was always interesting. All of these issues (reversals, transpositions, and omissions) were due to the dyslexia and created naming problems for different aspects of math, similar to those he showed in reading. Also, there were some mathematical concepts that Mike struggled with that related more to his fluency problems. For example, he struggled with word problems simply because he had trouble comprehending them because his poor reading fluency interfered with his understanding (as did his PA). When I made the teacher aware of the issues caused by the dyslexia, things were better for Mike in middle school (his teachers were always so responsive to his dyslexia, which is not always the case). And high school was even better because it was more conceptual and less detail oriented. Chemistry was a strength for Mike, whereas most students struggled with it.

A method I have used successfully to teach math facts and basic computation is called Touch Math (Independently published, 2019). I have also had great success by supplementing the regular school curriculum with homemade manipulatives. These included fraction pieces of different shapes (round, square, and rectangular) and lots of blocks and rods, not to mention pictures for almost everything.

Examples of homemade math manipulatives for fractions

More math manipulatives

Examples of handmade Touch Math numerals

Positive reinforcement is extremely important because it can offset the low self-esteem that these students often have. Praise should always be consistent, frequent, and sincere. Lots of positives are what these students with dyslexia need. They are very often overwhelmed with negative feedback, and as a result are often very sensitive.

PA is a gateway skill. So, it is important, but not at all the most important skill. That is why it is important to overemphasize strengths (in many cases, math) and underemphasize weaknesses (in many cases, PA). It is also extremely important to make sure students know if their dyslexia is affecting their math performance (which often is much less of an issue with higher level, conceptual and/or spatial math) or if they have a true math disability (which can last for the full academic time, into college and beyond).

> *A single act of kindness throws out roots*
> *in all directions, and the roots spring up and*
> *make new trees. The greatest work that kindness*
> *does to others is that it makes them kind themselves.*
> —Frederick William Faber, *Spiritual Conferences*

In other words, some students wrestle with a true math disability, which often is conceptual, and which can pervade the entire academic timeline for math. However, if a student has difficulties with PA, they will struggle in the early and mid-years of academic math, but be without problems later. This is because in lower and middle school, math is heavily about naming conventions, speed, and memorization, three challenges for students with dyslexia because these all are subject to problems with PA. But it is still important to address and overcome these issues by checking work multiple times (not fun) and going slowly (also not fun, especially if you have dyslexia and your brain moves very fast). But the early years of math are about speedy math facts, accurate memorization, and organization. Not until later, with more advanced math, can these students show off their higher-level thinking skills.

For Mike, math was harder in elementary and middle school because of his dyslexia. In high school math, he struggled more due to his ADHD. I did not work with Mike very much when he was in high school, so am unable to explore in detail about how his ADHD affected his math performance.

10 PHONOLOGICAL AWARENESS AND MATH

When we let go of all expectation, there is peace.

—Kim Eng

With its now broad and extensive literature that spans four-and-a-half decades, the role of phonological awareness (PA) in reading development is no longer in question.[1] In fact, Wagner and Torgesen claim that more is known about PA's relationship to reading than any other relationship to reading.[2] The more relevant questions around PA address the relationship between PA and academic outcomes other than reading and writing. The academic outcome most notably studied is math.

Many studies have uncovered an association between different PA tasks and math achievement.[3] Many of these same researchers found PA to be part of a broader construct of phonological processes, combining with several facets of memory (phonological and working) to contribute to automaticity of number and operation recall, and ultimately, math achievement.[4] Thus, there is support in the literature for phonological processes as a common cognitive pathway between reading and math computation.[5]

It has also been suggested that PA contributes to mathematics because it involves the retrieval and retention of verbal number codes.[6] When solving math problems, terms of a math problem may be first translated into speech-based codes, then processed by retrieving the verbal answer code for the respective math problem from long-term memory,[7] then again converted into an Arabic term.

Specific examples within mathematics of this verbal code processing include retaining and applying signs, symbols, and positions of numbers in a computational problem, conceptualizing number/quantity associations, which require specific symbol to concept recognition, and counting, which requires remembering the previous number, then identifying the next number in a sequence. All of these aspects of mathematics are directly affected by the automaticity a child has with the phonological name codes of numbers.[8]

Simmons and Singleton's phonological representations hypothesis suggests that all skills related to phonological processes should affect all aspects of math that involve a verbal code of some kind.[9] Krajewski and Schnieder found that PA deficits only affect the acquisition of verbal codes needed early on in math development (e.g., number words and counting), but if compensated for, do not affect verbally mediated higher-level math concepts.[10]

Robinson, Menchetti, and Torgesen attribute deficiency in math to either phonological processes or weakly developed number sense, with phonological processes having a more severe effect on fact recall.[11]

Geary speculated that there are three subtypes for math disabilities:

- Subtype 1 includes students who struggle with fact recall (speed and accuracy of facts and times tables), and basic arithmetic skills
- Subtype 2 involves difficulties with mathematical processes such as counting strategies, borrowing, and carrying
- Subtype 3 includes difficulties with visual spatial representation of numeric concepts

Geary speculates that only subtype 1 may be linked with phonologic deficits, noting that the left hemisphere and angular gyrus, the brain areas found to be atypical in individuals with dyslexia, may also be impaired in students with math disability. However, students with subtype 1 difficulties appear to demonstrate success with all other conceptual aspects of math (such as place value, subitizing, estimation).[12] Working with both normally developing children and those with disability, LeFevre and colleagues identified three pathways to math competence similar to Geary's: linguistic, quantitative, and spatial attention. Like Geary, LeFevre and colleagues hypothesize that linguistic skills predict performance on tasks involving symbolic representations (e.g., naming numbers, writing Arabic digits), while quantitative skills predict numeracy-related processes like part-whole comparisons, and spatial skills predict math skills more generally, affecting both of the numeracy-related and code-related skills described above, as well as visual-spatial working memory.[13]

In conclusion, there is substantial and growing evidence that the development of mathematical skills, particularly calculation, stems from multiple components, including PA. While calculations are numeric skills, they are also connected to linguistic abilities. Strengths and weaknesses in the code-related aspects of language and literacy thereby have respective influence on such calculations. There is still work to be done to uncover the exact role of PA and general math, though it does appear less associated with higher level conceptual math (e.g., math quantity understanding and prediction) and more associated with basic numerical skills (number words isolated from quantities). Similar to its role in reading, PA can be viewed as a necessary but not sufficient precursor to the development of math concepts and skill, influencing the ability to acquire and become automatic with number word identification and sequence.

The pause is as important as the note.
—Truman Fisher

PART TWO • DYSLEXIA AND ADHD

11 DESCRIBING ADHD

*In the midst of movement and chaos, keep
stillness inside of you.*
—Deepak Chopra

When Mike was in the middle of his ninth-grade year, I had a massive, cerebellar, hemorrhagic stroke. After brain surgery, I was sent to rehabilitation eight hours away. When I came home five months later, I had made some progress (regaining my breath, voice, and cognition) but still had a long way to go (I still could not swallow, walk, or use my hands). I left home (and my three daughters) again, to get more rehabilitation. This was when I met Steve. I knew he was special somehow. He was in charge of attaching and then keeping an electrical charge to the motor cortex in my brain. This sounds scary but Steve was masterful at keeping me calm and actually laughing. Soon after we began rehabilitation, he told me about his attention-deficit hyperactivity disorder (ADHD) and his school journey.

Although, as Mike's assessment indicated (see Appendix B), he also had ADHD, my focus with him was on his dyslexia. The timing of my stroke prevented me from continuing with Mike's tutoring into his high school years, when his ADHD might have been more of a focus for us.

What Is ADD or ADHD?

Often accompanying dyslexia is attention-deficit hyperactivity disorder (ADHD or ADD). This diagnosis is indicated by severe problems with attention, impulsivity, and/or hyperactivity across a variety of settings. People can think that because someone may have trouble focusing in math class, that person must have ADHD. Wrong! ADHD and dyslexia are similar, in that ADD, often now used interchangeably with ADHD, is the most common neurobehavioral disorder of childhood, and among the most prevalent chronic health conditions affecting school-aged children. ADD is characterized by inattention, including increased distractibility and difficulty sustaining attention; poor impulse control and decreased self-inhibitory capacity; and sometimes motor overactivity and motor restlessness.

Students with ADHD will often have no problem doing the homework, but will struggle to remember to turn it in. It is important to note that in individuals with ADHD, treatments can be helpful, but the ADHD will never be "cured." Also, the attentional and energy differences are chronic, and symptoms can last up to a lifetime. ADHD requires a medical diagnosis and a very small percent of people actually get diagnosed with ADHD. Many think they have it, but it may not be severe enough to be diagnosed, or it may not cut across contexts. Causes and risk factors are currently unknown, although we do know that genetics plays a role. While researchers know now that environmental conditions such as poor diet, poverty, or poor parenting do not cause ADHD, they know that they can certainly make it worse.

Ways to improve reading in children with ADHD include the following:

- Promote "pencil" facilitation, due to metacognition issues (this includes handwriting, which can often be quite illegible).
- Teach children with ADHD about ADHD (this will allow for self-advocacy—so important for individuals with dyslexia or ADHD).
- Develop self-monitoring strategies for before, during, and after reading (these will allow students to tell when they are paying attention and when they are not, without drawing public negativity to them).
- Learn to stop and ask questions to check for understanding along the way. This is essential.
- Use graphic organizers (these are like story webs or wheels and can take many different forms; see Chapter 6). They can be used to accommodate many different styles for the purpose of assisting organization in reading, writing, or comprehension.

Because of differences in the brain, individuals with either ADHD or dyslexia—or both—must work harder than most to accomplish the same task. They may seem to be avoiding work, but in fact may be overwhelmed or exhausted by it. It makes sense for the teachers to give more breaks and additional time to get work completed. Specific instruction in comprehension includes:

- Semantics (understanding the correct and accurate meaning of what is presented or within the student's writing)
- Sequencing (understanding the correct and accurate order of what is presented or within the student's writing)
- Main idea (This, along with the following four bullets, is often hard for the student with ADHD because of difficulty with organization and difficulty attending to details).

- Fact and opinion
- Cause and effect
- Instruction in mental imagery such as the Lindamood-Bell Visualizing and Verbalizing Program for Language Comprehension & Thinking[1]
- Give multiple opportunities to practice

Diagnosing ADHD with the DSM-V

DSM-V criteria for diagnosing ADHD include:

Hyperactivity/Impulsivity:(A2)

- Fidgets or squirms excessively
- Leaves seat when inappropriate
- Runs about/climbs extensively when inappropriate
- Has difficulty playing quietly
- Often "on the go" or "driven by an inconsistent motor"
- Persists for at least 6 months to a degree
- Talks excessively
- Blurts out answers before question is finished
- Cannot await turn
- Interrupts or intrudes on others' activities
- Inattention across multiple contexts.

For the full text of the DSM-V on ADHD, see Appendix A.

Diagnosing ADHD: Additional Important Comments:

- Several inattentive or hyperactive-impulsive symptoms are present prior to age 12.
- Several inattentive or hyperactive-impulsive symptoms are present in two or more settings.

- There must be clear evidence of clinically significant impairment in social, academic, or occupational functioning.
- Symptoms do not occur exclusively during the course of a pervasive developmental disorder, such as schizophrenia, or other psychotic disorder, and are not better accounted for by another mental disorder (e.g., mood disorder, anxiety disorder, dissociative disorder, personality disorder).

Other Facts about ADHD (all of which are not required for a diagnosis of ADHD)

- Attention to detail is problematic, makes many careless errors, has difficulty sustaining attention
- Fails to follow through / fails to finish instructions or schoolwork
- Avoids tasks requiring mental effort
- Often loses items necessary for developmental level and that negatively impacts completing a task
- Easily distracted which impacts directly on social and academic / occupational activities
- Tends to yawn a lot to help stay alert and focused

12 STEVE AND ADHD

I give you this to take with you: nothing remains as it was.
If you know this, you can begin again, with pure
joy in the uprooting.
—Judith Minty, *Letters to My Daughters*

Dyslexia and attention-deficit hyperactivity disorder (ADHD) both occur in the brain. About three in ten individuals with dyslexia are likely to have ADHD and an individual who has ADHD is six times more likely to have dyslexia as well. The brain with dyslexia and the brain with ADHD are different physically and chemically compared to that of an individual who is normally developing. The neurotransmitters do not work as efficiently in individuals with ADHD, and individuals with dyslexia often have less active left hemispheres.

Interview with Steve

I interviewed Steve about his experiences in high school and college as a student with ADHD. At the time this book was written, Mike had just finished high school, and was about to start college. Therefore, I was thrilled when Steve agreed to be interviewed about his high school and college experiences for my book. The following is drawn from our interview.

When were you first diagnosed with ADHD and how did they diagnose you?

Steve believes he was diagnosed with ADHD in second or third grade. He doesn't remember a lot of the specifics but does remember a lot of psychiatrists. He had a fair number of neurologic issues growing up, was given some psychoeducational evaluations, and was diagnosed with ADHD and other conditions. He had another evaluation right before he went to college.

As Steve told me, "ADHD is one of the most hereditary learning differences you can have." Steve's mom had it so there wasn't a huge stigma. He said he had more trouble dealing with the more symptomatic or behavioral elements of ADHD. That was what caused the tension.

High school for Steve was a mixed bag. Socially he started coming more into his own in high school. Middle school had been a bit of a nightmare struggling with social cues and that kind of thing.

And in high school Steve achieved quite a bit of success. He was a two-time national debate champion and for his state he was also quite successful. He was nationally very competitive in debate, which was "kind of a high-profile thing." BUT he struggled with schoolwork and had a great deal of trouble staying organized. Steve wouldn't turn in any of the homework and his grades always hovered around a C or C-.

So you mentioned having trouble with organization. Did this follow you into college?

In college, Steve really struggled. His family provided a lot of structure for him in high school—and he only understood how helpful it was when he went to college, and noticed its absence. His first attempt at college ended up not working out. In college he just did not have that kind of structure or motivation or ability around him, so he struggled to know how to start and lead work on his own. This is something everyone grapples with, but for him it was particularly hard. Steve ended up failing out during the first year of college.

After that, Steve spent a summer and a semester living with his parents, which was a very difficult experience. He did a lot of odd jobs around the house, but he doesn't think his parents knew what to do with him either. For about a month, he worked at a pizza place/bar from about 6 pm to 3 am. It was miserable.

Steve does not have siblings who also have ADHD. It's just him. He has an older brother and a younger sister. They both work in the non-profit world. Following are excerpts from a telephone conversation we shared, discussing Steve's higher education journey. My questions are bolded.

> **You went to Landmark College, didn't you?**
> *"Yes. So, after my time at home I decided to try college again and went to Landmark. Landmark was good, though socially quite isolating because it was in the middle of nowhere. There was not much to do which I think was part of the appeal—the stripping away of distractions was good academically. Yeah, it was good academically. It helped me in a variety of ways. It changed my mentality to one of self-determination. It changed to a focus on what I could do, not what my*

teacher did, etc. It was more of an attitude shift which was what I needed. It was good for my skills like organization which I am still not great at."

You are in good company with that!
"Yeah, to be honest I still have organizational deficits. But the bad parts of that are counteracted by a busy mind, thinking about what could or could not go wrong."

And now is so hard because the world is so small and we have access to everything at our fingertips so organization is harder now than it used to be.
"Yeah. 100%."

So did you ultimately graduate from Landmark or what happened?
"No I ultimately transferred out. Landmark as an institution is designed to be transferred out of. But it really helped me deal with my weaknesses. Part of me wishes that I had a degree from there because they helped me be successful at my next institution."

Is there anything else you'd like to add?
"No, just that ADHD can sometimes bring with it hidden strengths. For me that was being a good conversationalist and debater."

13 HOW TO RETEACH STUDY SKILLS

Sticking with uncertainty, getting the knack of relaxing in the midst of chaos, learning not to panic—this is the spiritual path.
—Pema Chödrön, *When Things Fall Apart*

Teaching study skills is hard, but it must and can be done. Teaching these skills to teenagers is hard enough...but add a little dyslexia or attention-deficit hyperactivity disorder (ADHD) to the mix and...oh boy! Teaching study skills becomes very hard, but not impossible. Whether you are a teacher, parent, researcher, or student you may find yourself feeling overwhelmed by assignments, to the point of laughing or crying, or simply exclaiming, "What were they thinking?". Many study skills are challenging for many students and I cannot begin to cover all of the relevant skills that students need to be successful. But in this chapter, I will cover those particular study skills with which my students have had the most success.

Organization

It gets harder to be organized as the world gets smaller and students have more and more access to information at their fingertips. I've seen this with all kinds of students: those with and without dyslexia or ADHD. The best way to approach organization is to narrow your focus. I do this by dividing organization into three sections: physical, mental, and temporal. These are very intuitive and students can get creative with them. I also like students to individualize these three categories of organization. For example, for physical organization, students must decide how neat their desk should be so that they can be most effective. With mental organization, students must know what kind of learner they are. Then they will know how best to memorize information for a test. With temporal organization, students will need to know how to write down their homework, so that they can read it and remember to do it (remembering to turn it in is a whole other skill). It could be a formal agenda book or a small notebook—whatever works well for each individual student.

I use a lot of checklists, because I tend to have success with them, and they can be quite metacognitive, thus requiring that students have the ability to think about things objectively, from a distance and at times, sequentially. For example, my Bookbag and Binder Checklist makes sure that students stay on top of the stuff—like their binder—that they need for school, and also get organizational help with the bookbag. We know how messy these bookbags and backpacks can get, especially if they are not recalibrated daily. In addition, students often need physical and organizational help with homework. This is where a tutor or teacher can personalize the approach and make a checklist that is unique to each student. For example, my evening checklist for Mike (see below) works because it is personalized as well as specific and measurable. It addresses the areas that he struggles with, in terms of getting homework done and put in the right place to be found and turned in the next day, which is not so easy for the student with dyslexia or ADHD. (As his assessment showed [see Appendix B], Mike had both.)

FUN-R

EVENING
CHECKLIST
For Mike to be prepared for school

1. Have all my homework done and checked by parent.

2. Put all homework into the accordion folder.

	1	2	3	4	5	6	7	8	9	10	11	12	13	14
English														
History														
Math														
Science														
Other														

3. Put accordion folder on the foot cushion in my room.

4. PLUG IN IPAD!

5. Make sure all the materials I'll need for school are together and on the foot cushion:

   ☐ Binder

   ☐ Accordion folder

   ☐ iPad

   ☐ Relevant books

 FUN-R (Foundation Underlying New Reading) · Elizabeth Cottone PhD

Mike's daily Evening Checklist, to be prepared for school the next morning.

AFTER-HOMEWORK CHECKLIST

FUN-R

DATE:	YES	NO
1. Did I have a planned study time?		
2. Did I tell my friends not to call me during my study time?		
3. Did I start working on time?		
4. Did I review my notes before beginning an assignment?		
5. Did I complete my hardest assignment first?		
6. Did I ask for help or call a "study buddy" when I got stuck on something?		
7. Did I finish one assignment before going on to another?		
8. Did I take short breaks when I felt tired?		
9. Did I avoid daydreaming?		
10. Did I write down questions to ask my teacher tomorrow in school?		

 FUN-R (Foundation Underlying New Reading) · Elizabeth Cottone PhD

The daily After-Homework checklist encourages the student to think objectively about the work they have just completed for school.

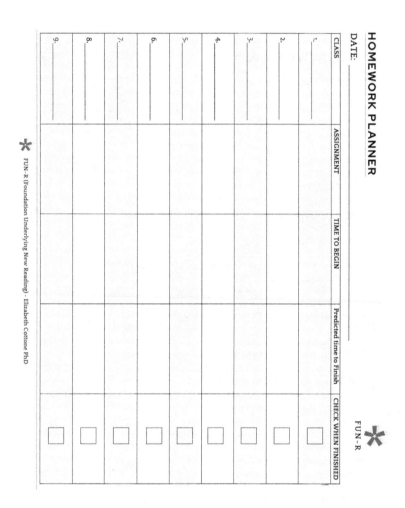

The Homework Planner provides checkboxes indicating completion of each assignment.

Memory Strategies

With mnemonic (or memory) strategies, you tie certain pieces of new or unfamiliar knowledge with old, familiar knowledge. This is like hanging new items of clothing on old hooks. These strategies are critical for students to learn directly, and I have used them successfully. They will affect students' performance on tests and quizzes as well as on class discussions. Many more mnemonic strategies exist (for others please see Scruggs and Mastropieri's article on mnemonic instruction[1]); here I'll discuss several that have worked well with my students. These include the Method of Loci, the Letter Strategy, the Keyword Strategy, and the Pegword Strategy.

Method of Loci (rhymes with slow-pie).

This is a mnemonic strategy for use when a student must memorize a list of unfamiliar terms. In order to memorize them, the student places each item in a familiar location that they know really well. I have had great success using the rooms in the student's house because they are so familiar. For example, if you must memorize the exports of India, you might first use your imagination and visualize putting a bag of rice in the dining room, as that is the first room you walk into when entering the house. Second, you might put henna in the downstairs bathroom, as that room is near the dining room on the same floor and it makes the most sense to put henna in that bathroom. The student continues in this way until all unfamiliar items are placed in a room.

Letter Strategy

With the Letter Strategy, a student will learn a list of unfamiliar or new words by taking the first letter of each new word and tying it to something familiar, like a list of friends' names. For example, the student may need to learn the ingredients in a brownie recipe, including butter, unsweetened chocolate, flour, sugar, eggs, and chocolate chips. So, the student visualizes their friends' names that start with the same letter as the ingredients. These include Ben, Ula, Frank, Sam, Ed, and Charlie.

FUN-R

LETTER STRATEGY

New List to Learn	First Letters	Names of Friends
Butter	**B**	Ben
Unsweetened chocolate	**U**	Ula
Flour	**F**	Frank
Sugar	**S**	Sam
Eggs	**E**	Ed
Chocolate chips	**C**	Charlie

FUN-R (Foundation Underlying New Reading) · Elizabeth Cottone PhD

The Letter Strategy links the first letters of familiar words with new words

By remembering this group of friends, the student can now remember all of the ingredients in the recipe, by matching each first letter together. The student then easily remembers the list of friends, because they are important people in the student's life.

Keyword Strategy

The Keyword Strategy is to be used when learning unfamiliar words, or with other information that is hard to remember. A keyword is a new word that sounds like the word to be learned and is easily pictured. It is helpful if the student creates a picture of the keyword and the new word doing something together. For example, if the new word is *ranidae*, which means common frog, the keyword could be rain and the picture could be a frog sitting in the rain. The keyword can help the student remember the new, unfamiliar word.

Pegword Strategy

The Pegword Strategy is used when information is in a sequence or order. This strategy taps visualization and connects the number word with a rhyming word that reminds the student of the step, event, or fact they are memorizing. To explain how it works, an example of this follows using a sequence from *Romeo and Juliet*:

One-bun—shooting guns (feuding between the Capulets and Montagues)

Two-shoe—Romeo and Juliet meet at a dance (picture Juliet wearing dancing shoes)

Three-tree—Tybalt wants revenge on Romeo (picture Tybalt hiding behind a tree)

Four-door—Romeo finds out that Juliet, his love, is a Capulet, part of the enemy's family (picture a door separating them)

Five-alive—Romeo and Juliet tell each other they are in love with each other (picture them both being alive with love)

Six-sticks—

Seven-heaven—

Eight-gate—

Etc.

Another example is if your student has to learn the seventh amend-
ment to the US Constitution (the right to trial by jury). The pegword
for seven is heaven so the student visualizes a heavenly, white-robed
jury in a white courtroom on a cloud.

> *Truth is ever to be found in simplicity,*
> *and not in the multiplicity and confusion of things.*
> —Isaac Newton

Test-Taking Strategies

Test-taking and prepping strategies are very important for students
with dyslexia. There are three ways to prepare for and take a test.

Remember the information that will be on the test.

We covered this when we talked about mnemonic strategies, which can
be very helpful when remembering content for tests.

Manage time wisely.

This means that students should use their mnemonic strategies well in
advance of the day before the test. They should figure out realistically
when to begin preparing. This is harder than it sounds.

Use appropriate test-taking strategies.

These include the following:

1. Look over the whole test and make sure you know what kinds
   of questions are on it: True/false? Multiple choice? Short
   answer? Essay? Also, figure out how much time you will need
   for each section.

2. Read all directions on a test and underline the key words.
3. Outline essay questions before writing any response.
4. Mark out any answers you know are wrong so as to eliminate choices that may confuse you.
5. Don't spend too much time on any one question, especially those that you may not know. Come back to these later.
6. Use other test questions and answers to remind you about forgotten answers.
7. If you are unsure, go with your first choice.
8. Use common sense.
9. Proofread your entire test.
10. Think of what the answer might be before looking at the choices.
11. RELAX! We now know that anxiety blocks blood to the brain and good thinking.

Use an acronym strategy like LEAPS (L= Look over entire test first, E= Every question must be answered, A= Attend to the details of every question, P= Look for part of the answer in the question, and S= Study your answers for a second time) to help remember all of these guidelines.

14 EPILOGUE—MIKE AND STEVE

It is being honest about my pain
that makes me invincible.
—Nayyirah Waheed, *Salt*

As of this writing, Mike has been accepted at a prestigious private college in New England, which he'll attend for the next four years. He has gone to a respected private K-12 school in the mid-Atlantic area for the last 12 years.

At age 27, Steve is working at a highly regarded university as a Non-Invasive Brain Stimulation Technician. In two years, he wants to be in a PhD program working in research investigations that make a functional difference in people's lives.

15 CONCLUSIONS

*You'll have bad times, but it'll always wake you
up to the good stuff you weren't paying attention to.*
—Robin Williams, *Good Will Hunting*

Being Misunderstood

One similarity between individuals with dyslexia, attention-deficit hyperactivity disorder (ADHD), and those with stroke is the experience of being misunderstood. It happens to all three groups of people. This can cause not only pain, shame, stress, isolation, and sadness but also motivation, inspiration, and drive ... to improve. It's confusing ... nothing in this world is ever black and white. And this is no exception. Dyslexia, ADHD, and stroke recovery are long processes that require a huge commitment.

Trauma and Grief

Don't underestimate trauma and grieving as part of the healing process for dyslexia. It can be traumatic and grief-filled to be an individual with dyslexia. Some have even said having dyslexia is as traumatic as being sexually abused. And surviving a bad stroke is so painful that survivors may even be suicidal. Both circumstances are intense and require many different kinds of healing—physical, social, cognitive, and emotional. It is very hard to live in this world and be misunderstood as being something you are not; if those around you think you are stupid because of your voice, your difficulty processing information auditorily, or the lack of speed in response, then life can be frustrating and aggravating. Both stroke and dyslexia can cause this, which can be devastating. It can take a long time, but eventually—and hopefully—we will come to understand that each person has the ability to be the best person they can be, regardless of whether that person is socially, cognitively, physically, or emotionally unpopular or unaccepted.

The Need for Love and Compassion

Both individuals with dyslexia or ADHD, and stroke survivors have a stronger than typical need for love and compassion. This is due to their sensitivity and pain, which arise from the trauma they both have experienced. While all three do need to surround themselves with individuals who are smart and know about the brain—and specifically what is going on in their own—more importantly, they both need to feel validated. They need to know that their opinion not only matters, but that it is fully understood to be as brilliant as it truly is. Love and compassion allow others to empathize sincerely with the individual with dyslexia or ADHD and the stroke survivor, and to understand what they must go through every day. All groups are alike in their high level of sensitivity because of what they have gone through: the trauma, the misconception, the alienation, and the feeling of being different and alone.

Speak to people with love and compassion and you
have the ability to create great change in them.
—Matt Valentine, founder of Buddhaimonia

Loss

Dyslexia, ADHD, and stroke involve devastating loss. With dyslexia or ADHD, loss takes the form of social isolation and cognitive mismatch. People with dyslexia and those with ADHD often experience social isolation for a variety of reasons. First, these individuals may lack or be weak in social skills. Therefore, they may lag behind their peers socially. Second, these individuals may be so advanced cognitively that they may not fit in with the social norms of their peer group. Both of these can be harmfully isolating. Third, individuals with dyslexia or ADHD are often "splintery" which means that they have some cognitive—and sometimes social—areas that are strong and others that are very weak. This combination makes them isolate further. And finally, sometimes if someone has dyslexia or ADHD and is an introvert, they can be at a loss for companionship, which can lead to or result in isolation.

Stroke survivors also experience great amounts of loss. Because every person with stroke is different (like people with dyslexia) it is almost impossible to delineate all of the different kinds of loss that accompany stroke.

Cognitive Mismatch

Cognitive mismatch occurs frequently with individuals with dyslexia or ADHD, although they may try to hide it. People with dyslexia or ADHD are often smarter than their peers, although it may go unnoticed, and they may appear stupid, often playing this up or taking on the role of "class clown." Often, they are out-of-the-box thinkers who are more creative than most and more intuitive as well. But they often don't feel that way about themselves because they don't enjoy being different, especially in middle and high school.

———————

Individuals with dyslexia or ADHD and stroke survivors offer so much more than meets the eye...much, much more. I hope with this book to educate and inform more and more people about the silver linings inherent in the lives of people affected by dyslexia, ADHD, and stroke.

APPENDIX A
ADHD DEFINED BY THE DSM-V

DSM-5 Criteria for ADHD

People with ADHD show a persistent pattern of inattention and/or hyperactivity–impulsivity that interferes with functioning or development:

1. **Inattention: Six or more symptoms of inattention for children up to age 16 years, or five or more for adolescents age 17 years and older and adults; symptoms of inattention have been present for at least 6 months, and they are inappropriate for developmental level:**
2. Often fails to give close attention to details or makes careless mistakes in schoolwork, at work, or with other activities.
3. Often has trouble holding attention on tasks or play activities.
4. Often does not seem to listen when spoken to directly.
5. Often does not follow through on instructions and fails to finish schoolwork, chores, or duties in the workplace (e.g., loses focus, side-tracked).
6. Often has trouble organizing tasks and activities.

7. Often avoids, dislikes, or is reluctant to do tasks that require mental effort over a long period of time (such as schoolwork or homework).

8. Often loses things necessary for tasks and activities (e.g., school materials, pencils, books, tools, wallets, keys, paperwork, eyeglasses, mobile telephones).

9. Is often easily distracted.

10. Is often forgetful in daily activities.

11. **Hyperactivity and Impulsivity: Six or more symptoms of hyperactivity-impulsivity for children up to age 16 years, or five or more for adolescents age 17 years and older and adults; symptoms of hyperactivity-impulsivity have been present for at least 6 months to an extent that is disruptive and inappropriate for the person's developmental level:**

12. Often fidgets with or taps hands or feet, or squirms in seat.

13. Often leaves seat in situations when remaining seated is expected.

14. Often runs about or climbs in situations where it is not appropriate (adolescents or adults may be limited to feeling restless).

15. Often unable to play or take part in leisure activities quietly.

16. Is often "on the go" acting as if "driven by a motor."

17. Often talks excessively.

18. Often blurts out an answer before a question has been completed.

19. Often has trouble waiting their turn.

20. Often interrupts or intrudes on others (e.g., butts into conversations or games)

In addition, the following conditions must be met:

- Several inattentive or hyperactive-impulsive symptoms were present before age 12 years.

- Several symptoms are present in two or more settings, (such as at home, school, or work; with friends or relatives; in other activities).
- There is clear evidence that the symptoms interfere with, or reduce the quality of, social, school, or work functioning.
- The symptoms are not better explained by another mental disorder (such as a mood disorder, anxiety disorder, dissociative disorder, or a personality disorder). The symptoms do not happen only during the course of schizophrenia or another psychotic disorder.

Based on the types of symptoms, three kinds (presentations) of ADHD can occur:

- *Combined Presentation*: if enough symptoms of both criteria inattention and hyperactivity-impulsivity were present for the past 6 months
- *Predominantly Inattentive Presentation*: if enough symptoms of inattention, but not hyperactivity-impulsivity, were present for the past 6 months
- *Predominantly Hyperactive-Impulsive Presentation*: if enough symptoms of hyperactivity-impulsivity, but not inattention, were present for the past 6 months.

Because symptoms can change over time, the presentation may change over time as well.

Diagnosing ADHD in Adults

ADHD often lasts into adulthood. To diagnose ADHD in adults and adolescents age 17 years or older, only 5 symptoms are needed instead of the 6 needed for younger children. Symptoms might look different at older ages. For example, in adults, hyperactivity may appear as extreme restlessness or wearing others out with their activity.

For more information about diagnosis and treatment throughout the lifespan, please visit the websites of theNational Resource Center on ADHD, the National Institutes of Mental Health, and the International Dyslexia Association.

References

American Psychiatric Association: *Diagnostic and Statistical Manual of Mental Disorders*, 5th ed. Arlington, VA: American Psychiatric Association, 2013.

Centers for Disease Control, "Attention-Deficit/Hyperactivity Disorder (ADHD): Symptoms and Diagnosis of ADHD." Last updated September 21, 2020. https://www.cdc.gov/ncbddd/adhd/diagnosis.html.

APPENDIX B

MIKE'S PSYCHOLOGICAL AND EDUCATIONAL ASSESSMENT, ENTERING GRADE 7

Dear Educators:

I recently completed a psychological and educational assessment with Mike [Name]

Mike is a rising 7th-grader at [school]. Mike is an exceptionally bright student who has also long evidenced signs of multiple learning disorders, including dyslexia and executive dysfunction. His parents brought him for evaluation at the recommendation of his long-term tutor, support, and advocate, Dr. Elizabeth Cottone. From a young age, Mike has shown impressive ease in his ability to learn information and understand higher-order concepts. He has, with high-quality and extensive intervention, shown considerable improvement in certain academic skills (e.g., reading). Yet, numerous difficulties have persisted (e.g., with writing). In addition, with the heightened organizational demands of middle school, Mike has shown a worsening in day-to-day school performance. Though he is motivated, he often loses track of work that has been assigned; he also forgets to deliver work he has completed. Resulting failures have been discouraging and are weakening his confidence in himself as a student.

Assessment results underscore Mike's outstanding intellectual strengths and confirm diagnoses of Specific Learning Disorder, with Impairment in Reading (315.00) and Written Expression (315.2); Attention-Deficit/ Hyperactivity Disorder, Predominantly Inattentive Type, Moderate (314.00); and Developmental Coordination Disorder (315.4; in his instance, dysgraphia). He processes information slowly. Discrepancies in Mike's strengths and weaknesses are unusually pronounced, exceeding any I have seen in my 20+ year career. It is critical that adults who work with him have an understanding—and appreciation of—his learning profile, in order to challenge him at a level appropriate to his intellect while supporting his needs.

Based on the evaluation results, I recommend that Mike have formal accommodation at [school], including the following: extended time on tests/exams (up to 100 percent additional) together with small-group testing and extra breaks; computer use for written work (including tests/exams); and the ability to record answers directly on tests/exams instead of having to transfer them to a Scantron form. At [school], I further recommend that consideration be given to reducing the quantity of work Mike needs to complete if it is not necessary to his personal mastery of the skills and concepts involved. Ideally, assignments would be posted on-line and Mike would be able to submit work electronically. Mike also needs to be allowed to use spell-check and should not be penalized for misspellings. I support and encourage the use of other technologies, too (e.g., SmartPen/Notability, voice recognition software such as DragonSpeaks, audiobooks). Finally, I urge [school] to waive Mike's foreign language requirement under what in my opinion are extenuating circumstances. I will provide additional explanation of these recommendations following my summary of evaluation findings.

In addition to interview with Mike, his parents, and his tutor, the assessment included the following measures; testing was completed on 05-29-2014:

Behavior Assessment System for Children

- Self-Report of Personality
- Parent Rating Scales, completed by Mr. and Mrs. [Name]

Behavior Rating Inventory of Executive Function

- Self-Report Version
- Parent Form, completed by Mr. and Mrs. [Name]

Conners' Continuous Performance Test – Third Edition

Delis-Kaplan Executive Function System (Color-Word Interference, Tower, Trail Making)

Rey Complex Figure Test (Original Copy, Immediate Delay)

Thematic Apperception Test, Card 1

Woodcock-Johnson III, Normative Update

- Tests of Cognitive Abilities (Cognitive Fluency, Processing Speed)
- Tests of Achievement, Form B (Broad and Basic Reading, Math, and Written Language)

Testing Mike was highly enjoyable. He was good natured in his inter-actions and open to testing itself. He showed good intrinsic motiva-tion; he appeared to like the opportunity to challenge his thinking and problem-solving. He demonstrated self-awareness via comments on his work and in his use of compensatory strategies. His remarks bespoke a dry humor, too, as when he quipped that an item "look[ed] easy but looks can be deceiving." Mike completed verbal (spoken) measures with obvious facility. In comparison, he was noticeably less proficient when working with visual and hands-on materials. When nonverbal abilities were emphasized, he worked more slowly and with less success. He seemed to need to translate information into a language-based form (e.g., using word labels and depictions, narrating his thought processes). He provided additional structure for himself in a variety of forms. Mike also relied on compensatory strategies when completing attention-related measures (e.g., shutting his eyes to reduce distractions, repeating information to himself). He showed overt behaviors suggestive of attention/executive function difficulties: He yawned and sprawled on the desk as if it was difficult for him to remain alert; there were times when he seemed to become lost in thought; he tapped his fingers or nibbled on them; he fidgeted with objects; he made sound effects as he worked; and he was sometimes impulsive (e.g., beginning work prior to hearing the directions, making seemingly detail-oriented mistakes). Despite his verbal strengths and consistent with both ADHD and dyslexia, Mike was often dysfluent in his speech and spoke haltingly. He used hand gestures to augment his communication, and he occasionally misspoke (e.g., saying *chandelabra* instead of *chandelier* or *candelabra*). He would also change direction mid-utterance. Associative thinking caused him to veer off-task on several occasions as when, after telling me that two creatures were both in the animal kingdom, he spontaneously rattled off "Phylum, Class, Order, Genus, Species." With these many factors at play, Mike's work pace was slow overall and he showed more fatigue than is usual. He needed more time than is usual to complete the standard cognitive and educational batteries. Yet, he continued to apply himself. Though they need to be interpreted within the context of these observations, results are believed to provide meaningful information about Mike's abilities and different influences on his performance.

Assessment Results

Evaluation of Mike's intellectual abilities was completed using the Wechsler Intelligence Scale for Children – Fourth Edition. The WISC-IV provides information about higher-order thinking abilities and processing in language-based and nonverbal areas. Subtests incorporate a variety of spoken, visual, and hands-on materials. Results are grouped into four indices: Verbal Comprehension (VCI), Perceptual Reasoning (PRI), Working Memory (WMI), and Processing Speed (PSI). Ordinarily, a composite score is provided in the form of a Full Scale IQ. However, with the marked variability that characterizes Mike's learning profile, a single number is wholly inadequate. Index and subtest scores provide more useful information about his strengths and weaknesses.

Wechsler Intelligence Scale for Children – Fourth Edition
Composite score mean=100, standard deviation=15

Subtest score mean=10, standard deviation=3

Verbal Comprehension		148	**Perceptual Reasoning**		----
Similarities	18		Block Design	10	
Vocabulary	17		Picture Concepts	17	
Comprehension	19		Matrix Reasoning	11	
(Information	16)				
Working Memory		102	**Processing Speed**		78
Digit Span	10		Coding	5	
Letter-Number Sequencing	11		Symbol Search	7	

On the Verbal Comprehension Index Mike earned a score of 148 (CI 139-151[*]), which places his measured verbal abilities in the *Very Superior* range, at the 99.9th percentile for his age. Outstanding as it is, there is a good likelihood that this score underestimates his strengths; though the WISC-IV is designed for use with students through age 16 and Mike is only 12, the test did not provide ample challenge. Mike continued to provide good quality answers through the end and did not meet the discontinue criterion on any of the subtests. Subtests measure both acquired knowledge and reasoning, Mike identified and explained the similarities in increasingly dissimilar pairs of objects or concepts (Similarities); defined concrete and abstract words (Vocabulary); provided the rationale underlying daily conventions or actions to take in given situations (Comprehension); and, on a supplemental test given as an introduction to testing, answered factual questions (Information). Mike's abilities are consistently developed at an advanced level. He has an impressive knowledge base, and he shows sophistication and depth in his understanding. His reasoning abilities are profoundly strong.

Mike's Perceptual Reasoning Index was not computed because of notable unevenness in his subtest scores, but results confirm that he is significantly less adept in his work with nonverbal materials than would be expected given his strong verbal intelligence. On the nonverbal subtests, Mike copied abstract geometric designs using red and white blocks (Block Design); chose from an array of pictures ones that were categorically related (Picture Concepts); and completed visual analogies (Matrix Reasoning). He did quite well on Picture Concepts which, of the subtests, most lends itself to language-based strategies and does not involve visual-spatial information. However, less interpretive weight is given to his high score because the subtest loads poorly on the index. In contrast, Block Design and Matrix Reasoning are more closely aligned with the primary constructs being measured, and Mike had notable difficulty on both. He had a hard time discerning spatial orientation, and he needed to work to analyze the materials as opposed to grasping them more intuitively. With the blocks, there were times when he narrated the placement of each one ("This needs to be a whole one"); he used logic to support his problem solving ("It's 3 by 3") instead of just knowing the configurations. With the matrices, he made detail-oriented and possibly impulsive mistakes on early items. He improved toward the end as he became more familiar with the task and harnessed his problem-solving abilities but he still had difficulty with items that were more spatially based. Difficulties with visual-spatial thinking are associated with disorganization.

On the Working Memory Index, Mike earned an *Average* score of 102 (CI 95-108; 55th percentile). Working memory involves the storage and use of information in short-term memory; an attention-related process, it provides a necessary foundation for any multistep task. Difficulties, even when comparative, have impacts. Mike's VCI>WMI discrepancy is also significant and unusual, with an expected occurrence of under 5 of every 1000 students. On the auditory tasks that make up the scale, Mike repeated increasingly lengthy series of numbers in forward and reverse sequence (Digit Span) and reordered mixed series of letters and numbers (Letter-Number Sequencing). He showed notable inconsistency across these, missing and answering items that are supposed to be of equal difficulty. His difficulties suggest that his weaknesses are compounded by problems with attention management.

Mike's Processing Speed Index of 78 (CI 73-88; 42nd percentile) is extremely low for someone with his verbal strengths, with a 40-point or greater VCI>PSI discrepancy expected in only 5 of 1000 students and his discrepancy being a full 70 points. (The table that provides discrepancy rates stops at 40 points.) His score is also lower than expected given his nonverbal and working memory abilities, and it is delayed for his age as well, in the *Low Average to Well Below Average* range. On the pencil-paper activities involved, Mike had to copy symbols, pairing them with numbers according to a code (Coding); he scanned rows of symbols, marking Yes or No depending on whether he located one of two target symbols (Symbol Search). Even though he worked slowly, he made errors. It is important to note that slower processing adds to demands on both attention and working memory.

Rey Complex Figure Test

Time to Copy	Within Normal Limits	Original Copy	$\leq 1^{st}$ percentile
		Immediate Delay	10th percentile

Additional information about Mike's nonverbal abilities was obtained using the Rey Complex Figure Test, on which he had to copy a single intricate figure. Without advance notice, he then had to copy it three minutes later from memory. Mike worked neither slowly nor quickly on the Rey, which involves both spatial organization and motor integration. His copies were both recognizable, but numerous lapses in motor control (e.g., with overshoots) and inaccuracies in placement of individual components contributed to an Original Copy score that is well below expectations for his age. That he showed improvement on the Immediate Delay suggests that memory *per se* is not a weakness.

Woodcock-Johnson III, Tests of Cognitive Abilities
Standard score mean=100, standard deviation=15

Processing Speed	70	Cognitive Fluency	80
Visual Matching	63	Retrieval Fluency	90
Decision Speed	88	Decision Speed	88
		Rapid Picture Naming	80

Further testing of Mike's processing efficiency shows that reductions extend to both language-based and nonverbal areas though they are most pronounced when the emphasis is on visual processing. Testing was completed using overlapping scales from the Woodcock-Johnson III, Tests of Cognitive Abilities. On these, Mike scanned rows of numbers and circled pairs (Visual Matching); listed examples of speci-fied categories (Retrieval Fluency); located and circled pairs of pictures that "go together" (Decision Speed); and named pictures of familiar objects (Rapid Picture Naming). Mike's *Well Below Average to Extremely Low* Processing Speed score of 70 (CI 63-78; 2nd percentile) needs to be interpreted carefully; he improved when he could use his reasoning abilities but was at the 1st percentile when he had to discriminate quickly among visual symbols. Though Cognitive Fluency involves both verbal and conceptual elements, Mike's score of 80 (CI 75-85; 9th percentile) remains below expectations for his age, in the *Low Average to Well Below Average* range. Naming speed has an attention/executive function component.

Conners' Continuous Performance Test – Third Edition

Formal testing of Mike's attention/executive functioning was completed using a variety of measures. On the Conners' Continuous Performance Test – Third Edition, he had to monitor a computer screen for 14 minutes, hitting the spacebar each time a letter other than X appeared and refraining from hitting the space bar when the letter was X. He was evaluated in terms of his accuracy, speed, and consistency. Mike's performance was average or better in all regards. He did not show difficulties on this test, but its computer basis might have allowed him to play to his strengths (Minecraft aficionado that he is). Further, the CPT has been faulted for its high rate of false negative results, particularly with children whose intellectual abilities are strong. Additional testing of Mike's attention/executive functioning, with portions of the Delis-Kaplan Executive Function System (D-KEFS), captures inconsistencies and difficulties.

Delis-Kaplan Executive Function System (D-KEFS)
Score mean=10, standard deviation=3

Trail Making Test

Completion Times		*Contrast (Number-Letter Switching vs....)*	
Visual Scanning	5	Visual Scanning	11
Number Sequencing	10	Number Sequencing	6
Letter Sequencing	1	Letter Sequencing	15
Number-Letter Switching	6	Combined Number & Letter Sequencing	---
Motor Speed	10	Motor Speed	6
Combined Number & Letter Sequencing	---		

Color-Word Interference Test

Completion Times		*Contrast*	
Color Naming	5	Inhibition vs. Color Naming	8
Word Reading	9	Inhibition/Switching vs. Combined Naming & Reading	5
Inhibition	3	Inhibition/Switching vs. Inhibition	9
Inhibition/Switching	2		
Combined Naming & Reading	(7)		
Total Errors			
Naming	15th percentile		
Word Reading	25th percentile		
Inhibition	Scale score of 3		
Inhibition/Switching	Scale score of 6		

Tower

Total Achievement Score	13
Time-Per-Move Ratio	9
Move Accuracy Ratio	9

The Trail Making Test of the D-KEFS consists of 5 timed "conditions," all of which involve marking or connecting circled numbers or letters (or in one instance empty circles) arrayed randomly on booklets. First, Mike had simply to mark instances of numbers. Then, he had to connect the numbers in order, following which he connected the letters in alphabetical order. The next condition required him to alternate or "switch" between numbers and letters, in order (1-A-2-B, etc.). Last, he traced dashed lines connecting the circles. Switching, which involves mental flexibility, is the key condition; the others are there largely to provide base rates for comparison.

Consistent with results on other measures, Mike was not efficient with visual scanning. He also did not show a good sense of alphabetic order. He had to repeat the alphabet to himself as he worked. (It is one thing to be able to recite the alphabet, which he can do, and another thing, when given one letter, to know immediately which letter comes next.) In contrast, Mike was fully automatic with numerical sequencing. Motor speed was not an issue (instructions include that one is not to be precise.) Given inconsistencies in Mike's base speeds on the different components, it is hard to interpret the Switching and Contrast results. That his completion time on Switching is below average for his age suggests difficulties with mental flexibility and working memory, but this same score is simultaneously higher than expected given his number sequencing and lower than expected given his letter sequencing.

Similar inconsistencies in base speeds complicate interpretation of Mike's results on the D-KEFS Color-Word Interference test, but because they are less pronounced and more predictable the results on this test offer useful information about a key aspect of executive functioning. Color-Word Interference is a standardized version of the classic "Stroop Test," on which the names of colors are printed in incompatible ink colors and individuals have to quickly say the ink color instead of reading the color word. Because at Mike's age he cannot prevent himself from reading words that he sees, the task requires inhibition of an automatic response. An added challenge on the D-KEFS version is that on one condition, Mike had to alternate between giving the ink color and reading the word depending on the presence or absence of a visual cue.

Consistent with other information Mike showed delays in naming speed, and while his word reading speed was age-appropriate it was not at the level of his verbal intellectual strengths. Though his scores suggest that haste was not a factor, he made a greater number of errors than is usual. He slowed further on the Inhibition test, with a completion time that is below expectations for his age and is also slower than expected once his naming and reading speeds are taken into consideration. Despite the slowdown, he made an even greater number of mistakes. Results show that, when working under time pressures, Mike is error-prone and has difficulty inhibiting responses. On an additional note, Mike slowed negligibly when the switching component was included and showed improved accuracy; this result suggests it was not difficult for him to be flexible in his thinking.

On the Tower test, Mike had to rearrange disks on wooden pegs using as few moves as possible within a time limit to reach a target configuration. He was only allowed to move one disk at a time, and he could not put a larger one on top of a smaller one. The activity measures planning abilities and is dependent, too, on visualization. Mike completed the early items in the minimum moves possible, but then began to have more difficulty. He almost exceeded time limits on one item, on which he made 27 moves as opposed to the minimum of 9 required. Though he made use of what he had learned on the next item, he subsequently reached a tipping point. In all, he earned the lowest possible score (without failure) on 3 of the 9 test items. His earlier successes allowed him to obtain an above-average Total Achievement score but his lower Time-Per-Move Ratio and Move Accuracy Ratio scores show that the process was less straightforward than the higher Total Achievement score suggests by itself.

Behavior Rating Inventory of Executive Functioning (BRIEF)

T-score mean=50, standard deviation=10

Scores of 65 and above are interpreted as clinically significant

	Self	Parent		Self	Parent
Behavioral Regulation	49+	70	**Metacognition**	65+	79
Inhibit	49+	53	Initiate	---	82
Shift	52	81	Working Memory	60	73
Emotional Control	50	72	Plan/Organize	69	77
Monitor	53	---	Organization of Materials	56	69
			Task Completion/Monitor	65+	75

Mike and his parents provided information about behavioral symptoms of attention/executive dysfunction using the Behavior Rating Inventory of Executive Function (BRIEF). Items on the BRIEF include symptoms of ADHD but are broader in scope. Specific behaviors are rated in terms of "never," "often," and "almost always" being problems. The Metacognition scale relates more directly to task completion, including initiation, planning and organization, follow-through, and review of work for effectiveness. Most of the ADHD-Predominantly Inattentive Presentation symptoms are included on these scales, primarily under Working Memory. In contrast, the Behavioral Regulation scale pertains more closely to modulation of emotions and (behavioral) impulse control. The ability to adapt flexibly to changing demands is included, too. There are slight differences in the composition of the Self-Report and Parent Forms of the BRIEF, which is why some scores appear to be missing.

Though ratings were at different levels of intensity, both Mike and his parents rated him as having *Clinically Significant* difficulties with metacognitive aspects of executive function. With regard to ADHD symptoms, he often has great difficulty getting started with work and does not have the materials he needs; he is easily distracted and loses track of what he is doing; he underestimates the time needed to complete tasks; he is apt to make careless mistakes or is sloppy with work; he is forgetful; and he often does not finish long-term projects. Though organization of materials appears to be a less prominent difficulty, this is misleading: Mr. and Mrs. [Name] rated Mike as "often" showing *all* of the behaviors included on the scale; 69 is the highest possible score.

Ratings differed more significantly on the Behavioral Regulation scale. Mike rated himself in the average range on all subscales, which resulted in an average composite score. In contrast, his parents communicated prominent resistance to change on his part and a tendency to become "stuck" in his thinking; they also indicated that he shows greater reactivity and moodiness. These ratings contributed to a *Clinically Significant* composite. Neither Mike nor his parents see him as having notable difficulties with impulse control.

Testing of Mike's educational skills was completed using the Broad and Basic Reading, Math, and Written Language composites of the Woodcock-Johnson III, Tests of Achievement. Consistent with his combination of strong intellect and ADHD and learning disorders, Mike demonstrates his strongest skills when higher-order thinking is involved. In language arts, he remains weaker in his basic skills, and his fluency score are low across the board. Academic composites highlight this pattern. Broad Reading and Written Language composites are omitted because they would be misleading. Skill delays take on greater significance given the amount and quality of intervention Mike has had.

Woodcock-Johnson – III, Tests of Achievement, Form B
Normative Update
Composite score mean=100, standard deviation=15
Age-based scores; grade-based scores would be comparable

Broad Reading	----	**Basic Reading Skills**	**87**
Letter-Word Identification	88	Letter-Word Identification	88
Reading Fluency	81	Word Attack	88
Passage Comprehension	125		

Broad Math	**110**	**Math Calculation Skills**	**105**
Calculation	112	Calculation	112
Math Fluency	92	Math Fluency	92
Applied Problems	111		

Broad Written Language	----	**Basic Writing Skills**	**73**
Spelling	63	Spelling	63
Writing Fluency	82	Editing	84
Writing Samples	110		
		Written Expression	----
		Writing Fluency	82
		Writing Samples	110

Academic Skills   **84**
(Letter-Word Identification, Calculation, Spelling)
Academic Fluency   **81**
(Reading Fluency, Math Fluency, Writing Fluency)
Academic Applications   **118**
(Passage Comprehension, Applied Problems, Writing Samples)

On the reading subtests, Mike pronounced words in isolation (Letter-Word Identification); exercised his decoding skills by sounding out phonetically correct nonsense words (Word Attack); read brief, simple sentences under timed conditions and indicated his understanding of them by answering *Yes* or *No* (Reading Fluency); and showed his understanding of what he read by providing the missing word in written text (Passage Comprehension). His Basic Reading Skills score of 87 (CI 84-91; 20th percentile) places his sight-word vocabulary and use of phonics in the *Average to Low Average* range. When sounding out actual words Mike did not seem to make use of the likelihood that they would be familiar to him. Typically, when students get close to known words there comes a moment of recognition, but for Mike the sounds he joined remained divorced from his lexicon. In keeping with these difficulties, he read quite slowly; though the words and language involved were simple, his Reading Fluency score of 81(CI 74-88; 10th percentile) is in the *Low Average to Well Below Average* range. As is usual with dyslexia, Mike benefited from context and meaning. Though time was involved, he demonstrated *Superior* understanding, with a Passage Comprehension score of 125 (CI 115-135; 95th percentile).

Mike obtained an *Average to High Average* Broad Math composite score of 110 (CI 105-115; 74th percentile), and his Math Calculation Skills score of 105 (CI 98-111; 63rd percentile) is comparable. On the math subtests, he worked a variety of problems in traditional format, using basic and advanced skills (Calculation); completed single-digit addition, subtraction, and multiplication items under time pressures (Math Fluency); and used his conceptual abilities and skills to solve increasingly complex math word problems (Applied Problems). Consistent with the possibility of ADHD, Mike was less automatic with written math facts than is optimal. He nonetheless shows good computation skills, but the process was time-consuming. With the word problems, he made detail-oriented mistakes; his strong reasoning abilities notwithstanding, he was not able to work out solutions on items that are meant to be challenging yet within reach.

On the writing subtests, Mike completed a traditional spelling test (Spelling); identified and corrected errors in printed text (Editing); formulated simple sentences quickly, based on pictures and using words provided (Writing Fluency); and wrote lengthier sentences according to specified guidelines (Writing Samples). Mike's difficulties with spelling and mechanics are pronounced. His Spelling score of 63 (CI 55-71) is in the *Well Below Average to Extremely Low* range, at the 1st percentile for his age. On Editing, on which he earned a *Low Average* score of 84 (CI 77-91; 15th percentile), he benefited from his language abilities but did less well with spelling and punctuation. Difficulties were more pronounced with his own writing. When writing under time pressures, Mike capitalized only 2 of 18 sentences and omitted end punctuation on all of them. He did only slightly better on the untimed items. (Please note that these errors are *not* penalized; the Writing Fluency and Writing Samples subtests are primarily measures of written expression.) Such difficulties are typical with learning disorders and dysgraphia, and Mike also showed the handwriting issues that characterize the latter.

He wrote slowly, obtaining a *Low Average to Well Below Average* Writing Fluency score of 82 (CI 72-91; 11th percentile); nonetheless, his handwriting was notable for inconsistencies in letter size, spacing, and position on the line. Basic weaknesses aside, Mike has a good ability to communicate information on paper. Though he is not yet a 7th-grader, I had him complete the item set for Grades 7-12 and average adults; he had little difficulty and earned an *Average to High Average* Writing Samples score of 110 (CI 101-120; 75th percentile).

Summary and Recommendations

Mike is an innately curious 12-year-old boy who finds appeal in knowledge and possesses excellent reasoning abilities. These attributes notwithstanding and though he has had the support of his family as well as extensive one-on-one intervention, he has a longstanding history of learning difficulties. His academic work is notably inconsistent. Assessment results document numerous learning issues that interfere with his school performance. His profile is notable for the exceptionality of strengths and weaknesses. Cognitive test results place Mike's verbal intellectual abilities more than 3 standard deviations above the mean for his age, at the 99.9th percentile. He demonstrates profound strength in his understanding and conceptual abilities. In comparison, his nonverbal abilities are significantly less well developed. He processes visual information slowly and his spatial organization abilities are poor. When working with nonverbal materials he is reliant on language-based mediation strategies and problem-solving, which adds to the time involved. As is more common with this profile, Mike also shows clinically significant difficulties with attention/executive functioning. He meets the criteria for a diagnosis of ADHD, Predominantly Inattentive Presentation, Moderate (314.00; please see page 8 for specific symptoms). Processing issues accompany behavioral signs of ADHD. Despite his facility with words and language, he has a slow naming speed. He has dysgraphia, too (Developmental Coordination Disorder, 315.4). Handwriting is effortful and poor. Mike's work pace is slower overall. Impacts extend to academic skills as well as day-to-day performance. Though Mike does better with applied skills—which typically involve greater meaning and allow for use of higher-order thinking abilities—these remain at a delay for someone as intelligent as he. With language fundamentals, his skills are below expectations for his age and grade. Even with the improvements that have come with tutoring and through his own hard work, discrepancies in his intellectual strength and basic skills remain at the order of 4 and 5 standard deviations. He meets the diagnostic criteria for Specific Learning Disorder, with Impairment in Reading (315.00) and Written Expression (315.2); his profound spelling disability is subsumed under the latter. Under DSM-IV-TR criteria, which emphasized ability-achievement discrepancies, Mike would additionally have met the criteria for a Math Disorder, but the DSM-V criteria place great weight on age-based delays. He is less automatic with written math facts. Though his computation skills and problem-solving compare favorably to expectations for his age, it is likely that he will find math to be more difficult as spatial skills/concepts become increasingly central. Dr. Cottone reports that he has already had trouble with some topics.

Mike's combination of strengths and weaknesses poses rewards and challenges to him and to adults who work with him. Given his outstanding acumen for learning, it can be difficult for educators to grasp and keep in mind his need for support. Conversely, Mike is likely to focus on his difficulties and lose track of the strengths he possesses. He needs the opportunity to participate in accelerated courses that whet his learning and confidence; at the same time, he needs support.

Apropos the recommendations included at the beginning of the report: Mike needs extended time on test to offset time lost to attention lapses and slower processing, and to allow him sufficient opportunity to use compensatory strategies and double check his work. In addition, working under time pressures appears to elicit mistakes. Small-group testing is recommended to reduce distractions; it also allows him to move around with less distraction to others. He needs extra breaks because of the fatigue that comes with his learning profile; opportunities to revive are important to his alertness. Computer use is advisable because of his dysgraphia; the reduction of motor demands correspondingly leaves Mike with additional cognitive energy for thinking about the test questions and formulating his answers. Use of Scantron forms is inadvisable because of the motor precision required and the increased likelihood of recording errors. Mike's spelling skills are at the 1st percentile, and given the intervention he has it appears they are to a great extent intractable. Grappling with how to spell words comes at a cost to other aspects of writing and benefit to spelling itself is minimal. Mike needs to be able to use spell-check in part so that his writing is understandable to others; even with spell-check use, there will still be misspellings in his writing, and he should not be penalized for these because that would be in effect penalizing him for a disability.

It is my understanding that [school] has a new policy that does not allow for students to graduate without fulfilling a foreign language requirement. I am requesting that an exception be made for Mike. With his strengths, he has much to offer to [school] as well as much to gain from his education there. Yet—and this is a statement I do not make lightly—I do not feel that it is possible for him to pass a traditional foreign language course. Even with considerable intervention with a specialist, and participation in [other school]'s summer program, Mike's basic reading and writing skills remain weak in his native English. He is slower in his word retrieval, he shows an unusually poor ability to encode the sounds of language, and his ability to process visual symbols is reduced. All of these factors impinge on his ability to remember new letter patterns and to read and write with them. Further, there is the issue of "load." With his disabilities, Mike needs considerably more time than other students to complete work (which is why I am also recommending that consideration be given to reducing the quantity of work he is assigned as long as there is not an impact on mastery). Foreign language study would come at a great cost to other learning and to minimal avail.

It is also with the issue of load in mind that I recommended various technologies, including electronic posting/submission of assignments and use of compensatory tools such as a SmartPen/Notability, voice recognition software by Dragon Speaks, and audiobooks. (Though Mike devours books of his own choosing, reading skills and fluency can vary with the content and form of materials; narratives offer support that other types of works do not.) For Mike, the processing of information detracts from the strengths that are otherwise there; by minimizing demands on processing, he will have additional resources for higher-order thinking and problem-solving.

It is important to capitalize on Mike's strengths as these facilitate his confidence, motivation, and learning. In the classroom this will occur naturally with an emphasis on discussion and concepts. Other compensatory strategies include explicit structure and organization (e.g., well-established routines, straightforward templates/rubrics for projects); reduction of working memory demands (e.g., by breaking tasks into manageable components and providing information in written form); reduction in visual-motor demands (e.g., minimizing the need to copy from the board or textbook); and reinforcement and structure for work habits (e.g., reminders/reinforcement for filling out agenda books, binder checks).

I recommend that Mike continue to work with Dr. Cottone, as she "gets" Mike, makes tutoring enjoyable, conveys his strengths to him, has an array of skills to impart, and is a trusted support. In addition to focusing on individual skills in their work together, it will be important to build on Mike's work habits.

Structure and routines can be used to facilitate better organization and habits. Behaviors that are automatic are less susceptible to lapses in focus/working memory and are more likely to be completed. Good auto-pilots increase efficiency, not only in terms of time but also energy and other resources. Within the context of an organized system, however, it is likely that Mike will need variety in some form to keep his interest up. It can be a difficult balance to achieve: Enough familiarity, routine, and simplicity to promote automaticity and to keep Mike from having to reinvent the wheel, but sufficient novelty and complexity to maintain his initiative and engagement. Tedium is counterproductive in terms of attention. When providing structure, it is also important to avoid rigidity.

Behavioral principles can be used to develop and maintain adaptive habits. It is good to choose one or two habits to focus on at a time (e.g., keeping track of school materials); to come up with a simple plan (e.g., an accessible and visible place to them on arrival home from school and, once homework is done, ready for school departure in the morning); to give reminders at the outset to focus attention on the behavior (e.g., spoken cues from adults, a posted sign in the front hallway); and to provide reinforcement for successful completion of the behavior (e.g., praise when time materials are where they need to be and make it to/from school). Though students with Mike's profile often have great experiential memory (e.g., recalling details from a long-ago trip), they tend not to learn as quickly from experiences/consequences. Reinforcement is most successful when it occurs in close time proximity to the behavior. It can be eliminated gradually once the new habit is established, but periodic "boosters" are likely to be needed. As a side note, grades are typically less effective mechanisms for change because they occur at such a remove from the behaviors involved.

It will be important for Mike to give conscious attention to the conditions that optimize his focus and productivity when completing schoolwork. For example, he could plan to complete work that is less interesting or more difficult with those times of day when he is more alert. He might find it helpful to start with something quick and easily managed as a way of "priming the pump" and then proceed to something more challenging. Mike will likely find it easier to stay focused if he has increased opportunities for movement as he works. Exercising beforehand can increase alertness, too. Environmental factors are influential, including the degree of noise and background stimulation (e.g., proximity to others, music on or off). Optimal conditions will likely vary with the task, and it will be important for Mike to monitor his productivity and make changes as needed. If Mike is having difficulty initiating or completing work, he could make an agreement with himself to work for a short period—or until he finishes a certain portion—and then take a break. It can sometimes be useful to change tasks.

Attention and executive functions are disproportionately energy-intensive, which makes physical well-being of increased importance (e.g., through regular exercise, good nutrition, sound sleep). Ample opportunity for leisure is important as well. Mike needs considerable time for recharging and without it is apt to become moody and more easily frustrated.

A practical resource for attention/executive function weaknesses is the book *Smart but Scattered: The Revolutionary "Executive Skills" Approach to Helping Kids Reach Their Potential,* by Peg Dawson, Ed.D. and Richard Guare, Ph.D.[1]

I thoroughly enjoyed this opportunity to work with Mike and his family. I hope this information is useful to them and to everyone who works with Mike.

Julia Blodgett, Ph.D.
Licensed Clinical Psychologist

FURTHER READING

1. Sally Shaywitz, *Overcoming Dyslexia*, New York: Vintage Books, 2005.

2. Thomas G. West, *In the Mind's Eye: Creative Visual Thinkers, Gifted Dyslexics, and the Rise of Visual Technologies*. 2nd ed. Amherst, NY: Prometheus Books, 2009. West notes that Albert Einstein, Michael Faraday, James Clerk Maxwell, Sir Winston Churchill, Gen. George Patton, and William Butler Yeats all had some kind of LD.

3. Ruth Culham, *6+1 Traits of Writing: The Complete Guide Grades 3 and Up*. Portland, OR: Northwest Regional Educational Laboratory, 2003.

4. Charlotte G. Morgan, *When They Can't Write*. London: York Press, 2001.

5. Orton-Gillingham Academy, Amenia, NY. https://www.ortonacademy.org/.

6. Slingerland Institute for Literacy. Bellevue, WA. https://slingerland.org/.

7. Kristin Johnson. *Megawords 1-3*. 2nd ed. Cambridge, MA: Educators Publishing Service, 2010.

8. Kenneth U. Campbell. *Great Leaps Reading: Grades 6–8*. 5th ed. Gainesville, FL: Diarmuid, 2008. See also, "Reading Fluency." Great Leaps. https://greatleaps.com/collections/reading.

9. Dorothy Blosser Whitehead. *Dyslexia: Unlocking the Power of Print*. Portland, OR: published by the author, 1997.

10. International Dyslexia Association (IDA). https://dyslexiaida.org/. Both federal and state branches, as well as local resources, can be found from this website. The Virginia branch is at https://va.dyslexiaida.org/

11. LD Online. http://www.ldonline.org/

12. Council for Exceptional Children. Arlington, VA. https://exceptionalchildren.org/

ABOUT THE AUTHOR

Elizabeth Cottone, PhD, was a research scientist (Assistant Research Professor) for 11 years at The Center for Advanced Study of Teaching and Learning (CASTL), part of the University of Virginia's Curry School of Education. Her research interests include dyslexia, stroke, investigating pathways from economic disadvantage to poor outcomes for children, and understanding families in poverty through a resilience lens.

The author with Sassy the miniature donkey

In 2017, while transitioning to a new job, Cottone had a massive, life-threatening stroke, seemingly out of the blue. Since that time, she has been working hard to recover, trying to fully understand what it means to go slowly, and appreciating all the silver linings as she recognizes them, one by one.

Her FUN-R (Foundation Underlying New Reading) method incorporates her broad experience as a research scientist and as a tutor for students with dyslexia and other learning disabilities.

Beth Cottone has discovered similarities among stroke survivors like herself and people with dyslexia and ADHD, and works to support recovery and education for people with neurodivergent brains.

With former colleagues from the University of Virginia, James Kauffman and Jeanmarie Badar, she is drafting a paper for a new academic journal on the topic of human belonging. With another colleague, Cottone is spearheading an academic paper on resilience in marginalized communities.

Visit elizabethcottone.com for more information and to contact the author.

NOTES

Acknowledgments

1. Sally Shaywitz, *Overcoming Dyslexia* (New York: Vintage Books, 2005).
2. Thomas G. West, *In the Mind's Eye: Creative Visual Thinkers, Gifted Dyslexics, and the Rise of Visual Technologies*, 2nd ed. (Amherst, NY: Prometheus Books, 2009).

Preface

1. Steve A. Hecht, Joseph K. Torgesen, Richard K. Wagner, and Carol A. Rashotte, "The Relations between Phonological Processing Abilities and Emerging Individual Differences in Mathematical Computation Skills: A Longitudinal Study from Second to Fifth Grades," *Journal of Experimental Child Psychology* 79, no. 2 (2001): 192–227.
2. Hecht et al., "Relations"; Tuire Koponen, Kaisa Aunola, Timo Ahonen, and Jari-Erik Nurmi, "Cognitive Predictors of Single-Digit and Procedural Calculation Skills and Their Covariation with Reading Skill," *Journal of Experimental Child Psychology* 97, no. 3 (2007): 220–41; Carol S. Robinson, Bruce M. Menchetti, and Joseph K. Torgesen, "Toward a Two–Factor Theory of One Type of Mathematics Disabilities," *Learning Disabilities Research and Practice* 17, no. 2 (2002): 81–89.

How to Use This Book

1. Pseudonyms are used for Mike, his parents Emily and Keith, and for Steve.

1. Parents and Heritability

1. Ernest Boyer, "Public Law 94-142: A Promising Start?," *Educational Leadership* 36, no. 5 (1979): 300.
2. This wide range of competencies, from kindergarten to high school, indicated that Mike's dyslexia was more severe than Emily's.

2. What Is Dyslexia? Why Should We Care?

1. Shaywitz, *Overcoming Dyslexia*, 10.
2. "Definition of Dyslexia," International Dyslexia Association, adopted November 12, 2002, https://dyslexiaida.org/definition-of-dyslexia/.
3. Benita A. Blachman, "Relationship of Rapid Naming Ability and Language Analysis Skills to Kindergarten and First-Grade Reading Achievement," *Journal of Educational Psychology* 76, no. 4 (1984): 610–22; Christopher J. Lonigan, Stephen R. Burgess, Jason L. Anthony, and Theodore A. Barker, "Development of Phonological Sensitivity in 2- to 5-Year-Old Children," *Journal of Educational Psychology* 90, no. 2 (1998): 294–311; Beth M. Phillips, Jeanine Clancy-Menchetti, and Christopher J. Lonigan, "Successful Phonological Awareness Instruction with Preschool Children: Lessons from the Classroom," *Topics in Early Childhood Special Education* 28, no. 1 (May 2008): 3–17; Gary A. Troia, Phonological Awareness Intervention Research: A Critical Review of the Experimental Methodology," *Reading Research Quarterly* 34 (1999): 28–52.
4. Hecht et al., "Relations"; Stephanie Al Otaiba, Cynthia S. Puranik, Robyn A. Ziolkowski, and Tricia M. Montgomery, "Effectiveness of Early Phonological Awareness Interventions for Students with Speech or Language Impairments," *Journal of Special Education* 43, no. 2 (2009): 107–28.
5. Blachman, "Relationship of Rapid Naming Ability"; Lonigan et al., "Development of Phonological Sensitivity"; Jason L. Anthony and David J. Francis, "Development of Phonological Awareness," *Current Directions in Psychological Science* 14, no. 5 (2005): 255–59.
6. Anthony and Francis, "Development of Phonological Awareness"; Peter E. Bryant, Morag MacLean, Lynette L. Bradley, and J. Crossland, "Rhyme and Alliteration, Phoneme Detection, and Learning to Read," *Developmental Psychology* 26, no. 3 (1990), 429–38; Stacey A. Storch and Grover J. Whitehurst, "Oral Language and Code-Related Precursors to Reading: Evidence from a Longitudinal Structural Model," *Developmental Psychology* 38, no. 6 (2002): 934–47; Richard Wagner and Joseph K. Torgesen, "The Nature of Phonological Processing and Its Causal Role in the Acquisition of Reading Skills," *Psychological Bulletin* 101 (1987): 192–212.
7. Linnea C. Ehri, Simone Resende Nunes, Dale M. Willows, Barbara Valeska Schuster, Zohreh Yaghoub-Zadeh, and Timothy Shanahan, "Phonemic Awareness Instruction Helps Children Learn to Read: Evidence from the National Reading Panel's Meta-Analysis," *Reading Research Quarterly* 36, no. 3 (2001): 250–87; Linnea C. Ehri, Simone R. Nunes, Steven A. Stahl, and Dale M. Willows, "Systematic Phonics Instruction Helps Students Learn to Read: Evidence from the National Reading Panel's Meta-Analysis," *Review of Educational Research* 71, no. 3 (2001): 393–447; Phillips, Clancy-Menchetti, and Lonigan, "Successful Phonological Awareness Instruction"; Storch and Whitehurst, "Oral Language."
8. Joseph K. Torgesen, Ann W. Alexander, Richard K. Wagner, Carol A. Rashotte, Kytja K. S. Voeller, and Tim Conway, "Intensive Remedial Instruction for Children with

Severe Reading Disabilities: Immediate and Long-Term Outcomes from Two Instructional Approaches," *Journal of Learning Disabilities* 34, no. 1 (2001): 33–58.

9. Adriana Bus and Marinus van IJzendoorn, "Phonological Awareness and Early Reading: A Meta-Analysis of Experimental Training Studies," *Journal of Educational Psychology* 91, no. 3 (1999): 403–14; Ehri et al., "Phonemic Awareness Instruction"; Ehri et al., "Systematic Phonics Instruction."

10. Phillips. Clancy-Menchetti, and Lonigan, "Successful Phonological Awareness Instruction"; Christopher J. Lonigan, "Development and Promotion of Emergent Literacy Skills in Preschool Children At-Risk of Reading Difficulties," in *Preventing and Remediating Reading Difficulties: Bringing Science to Scale*, ed. Barbara R. Foorman (Timonium, MD: York Press, 2003), 23–50.

11. Stephanie Al Otaiba, Cynthia Puranik, Robin Zilkowski, and Tricia Montgomery, "Effectiveness of Early Phonological Awareness Interventions for Students with Speech or Language Impairments," *Journal of Special Education* 43, no. 2 (2009): 107–28; Phillips. Clancy-Menchetti, and Lonigan, "Successful Phonological Awareness Instruction."

12. Caroline Henning, Beth McIntosh, Wendy Arnott, and Barbara Dodd, "Long-Term Outcome of Oral Language and Phonological Awareness Intervention with Socially Disadvantaged Preschoolers: The Impact on Language and Literacy," *Journal of Research in Reading* 33, no. 3 (2010): 231–46.

13. Henning et al., "Long-Term Outcome"; Alex Nancollis, Barbara-Anne Lawrie, and Barbara Dodd, "Phonological Awareness Intervention and the Acquisition of Literacy Skills in Children from Deprived Social Backgrounds," *Language, Speech, and Hearing Services in Schools* 36, no. 4 (2005): 325–35; Robyn Ziolkowski and Howard Goldstein, "Effects of an Embedded Phonological Awareness Intervention during Repeated Book Reading on Preschool Children with Language Delays," *Journal of Early Intervention* 31, no. 1 (2008): 67-90.

14. Christopher Lonigan, Jason Anthony, Brenlee Bloomfield, Sarah Dyer, and Corine Samwel, "Effects of Two Shared-Reading Interventions on Emergent Literacy Skills of At-Risk Preschoolers," *Journal of Early Intervention* 22 (1999): 306–22.

15. "Dyslexia: Overview," Mayo Clinic, July 22, 2017, https://www.mayoclinic.org/diseases-conditions/dyslexia/symptoms-causes/syc-20353552.

16. Understood for All, accessed June, 2018, https://www.understood.org/.

17. Horowitz, S. H., Rawe, J., & Whittaker, M. C. (2017). *The State of Learning Disabilities: Understanding the 1 in 5.* New York: National Center for Learning Disabilities. https://ncld.org/research/state-of-learning-disabilities/.

18. Kristen Harper and Edward Fergus, "Policymakers Cannot Ignore the Overrepresentation of Black Students in Special Education," *Child Trends*, October 12, 2017, https://www.childtrends.org/blog/policymakers-cannot-ignore-overrepresentation-black-students-special-education; National Center for Education Statistics (NCES), https://nces.ed.gov/.

19. An Individualized Education Program (IEP) is a legally protected document that maps out the special education services and supports which a child—from age 5 through high school—is entitled to in a US public school.

20. A 504 plan is governed by federal civil rights law. It can mandate support, outside of the special education system, for students with disabilities, for example with accommodations like extra time on tests, or help with study skills.

21. Horowitz et al., *The State of Learning Disabilities.*

4. What Is LD and Where Does Dyslexia Fit in?

1. Individuals with Disabilities Education Act, Sec. 300.8 (c) (10), last modified May 25, 2018, https://sites.ed.gov/idea/regs/b/a/300.8/c/10.

5. Teaching Mike How to Read

1. Individuals with Disabilities Education Act, Sec. 300.8 (c) (10).

6. How to Reteach Reading

1. "Reading Fluency," Great Leaps, accessed August 14, 2021, https://greatleaps.com/collections/reading.

2. National Reading Panel, *Teaching Children to Read*, NIH Pub. No. 00-4769 (Washington, DC: U.S. Department of Health and Human Services, 2000).

3. Steven A. Stahl and Melanie R. Kuhn, Stahl, Steven & Kuhn, Melanie, "Making It Sound like Language: Developing Fluency," *Reading Teacher* 55, no. 6 (2002): 582–84.

4. Orton-Gillingham Academy, Amenia, NY, accessed August 14, 2021, https://www.ortonacademy.org/.

7. Mike and Writing

1. Ruth Culham, *6+1 Traits of Writing: The Complete Guide Grades 3 and Up* (Portland, OR: Northwest Regional Educational Laboratory, 2003).

8. How to Reteach Writing

1. Charlotte G. Morgan, *When They Can't Write* (London: York Press, 2001).

10. Phonological Awareness and Math

1. Anthony and Francis, "Development of Phonological Awareness"; Ehri et al., "Phonemic Awareness Instruction."
2. Wagner and Torgesen, "Nature of Phonological Processing."
3. Tracy Packiam Alloway, Susan Elizabeth Gathercole, Anne-Marie Adams, Catherine Willis, Rachel Eaglen, and Emily Lamont, "Working Memory and Phonological Awareness as Predictors of Progress towards Early Learning Goals at School Entry," *British Journal of Developmental Psychology* 23, no. 3 (2005): 417–26; Peter Bradley and Lynette Bryant, *Children's Reading Problems: Psychology and Education* (Oxford: Blackwell, 1985); Hecht et al., "Relations"; Koponen et al., "Cognitive Predictors"; Kristin Krajewski and Wolfgang Schneider, "Early Development of Quantity to Number-Word Linkage as a Precursor of Mathematical School Achievement and Mathematical Difficulties: Findings from a Four-Year Longitudinal Study," *Learning and Instruction* 19, no. 6 (2009): 513–26; Fiona Simmons, Chris Singleton, and Joanna Horne, "Brief Report--Phonological Awareness and Visual-Spatial Sketchpad Functioning Predict Early Arithmetic Attainment: Evidence from a Longitudinal Study," *European Journal of Cognitive Psychology* 20, no. 4 (2008): 711–22.
4. Alloway et al., "Working Memory"; Hecht et al., "Relations"; Koponen et al., "Cognitive Predictors."
5. David C. Geary, "Mathematical Disabilities: Cognitive, Neuropsychological, and Genetic Components," *Psychological Bulletin* 114, no. 2 (1993): 345–62; Byron P. Rourke and James A. Conway, "Disabilities of Arithmetic and Mathematical Reasoning: Perspectives from Neurology and Neuropsychology," *Journal of Learning Disabilities* 30, no. 1 (1997): 34–46; Chris Dollaghan and Thomas F. Campbell, "Nonword Repetition and Child Language Impairment," *Journal of Speech, Language, and Hearing Research* 41 (1998): 1136–46; Stanislas Dehaene, "Varieties of Numerical Abilities," *Cognition* 44, no. 1–2 (1992): 1–42; Axel Buchner, Melanie C. Steffens, and Rainer Rothkegel, "On the Role of Fragmentary Knowledge in a Sequence Learning Task," *Quarterly Journal of Experimental Psychology,* 51 (1998): 251–81; Axel Buchner, Melanie C. Steffens, Lisa Irmen, and Karl F. Wender, "Irrelevant Auditory Material Affects Counting," *Journal of Experimental Psychology: Learning, Memory, and Cognition* 24, no. 1 (1998): 48–67; Simmons, Singleton, and Horne, "Brief Report."
6. Dollaghan and Campbell, "Nonword Repetition"; Robinson, Menchetti, and Torgesen, "Toward a Two–Factor Theory."
7. David C. Geary, Mary K. Hoard, and Carmen O. Hamson, "Numerical and Arithmetical Cognition: Patterns of Functions and Deficits in Children at Risk for a Mathematical Disability," *Journal of Experimental Child Psychology* 74, no. 3 (1999): 213–39.
8. Rebecca Bull and Rhona S. Johnston, "Children's Arithmetical Difficulties: Contributions from Processing Speed, Item Identification, and Short-Term Memory," *Journal of Experimental Child Psychology* 65, no. 1 (1997): 1–24; Hecht et al., "Relations"; Krajewski and Schneider, "Early Development"; Rourke and Conway, "Disabilities of Arithmetic."

9. Fiona R. Simmons and Chris Singleton, "Do Weak Phonological Representations Impact on Arithmetic Development? A Review of Research into Arithmetic and Dyslexia," *Dyslexia* 14, no. 2 (2008): 77–94.
10. Krajewski and Schnieder, "Early Development."
11. Robinson, Menchetti, and Torgesen, "Toward a Two–Factor Theory."
12. Geary, "Mathematical Disabilities."
13. Jo-Anne LeFevre, Lisa Fast, Sheri-Lynn Skwarchuk, Brenda L. Smith-Chant, Jeffrey Bisanz, Deepthi Kamawar, and Marcie Penner-Wilger, "Pathways to Mathematics: Longitudinal Predictors of Performance," *Child Development* 81, no. 6 (2010): 1753–67.

11. Describing ADHD

1. Nanci Bell, Visualizing and Verbalizing Program for Language Comprehension & Thinking. https://ganderpublishing.com/pages/visualizing-and-verbalizing-overview.

13. How to Reteach Study Skills

1. Thomas E. Scruggs and Margo A. Mastropieri, "The Effectiveness of Mnemonic Instruction for Students with Learning and Behavior Problems: An Update and Research Synthesis," *Journal of Behavioral Education* 10, no. 2–3 (2000): 163–73.

Appendix B

1. Peg Dawson and Richard Guare, *Smart but Scattered: The Revolutionary "Executive Skills" Approach to Helping Kids Reach Their Potential* (New York: Guilford Press, 2009).

CPSIA information can be obtained
at www.ICGtesting.com
Printed in the USA
BVHW041935311021
620410BV00015B/712